NORTHERN OHIO LEGENDS & LORE

JAMES A. WILLIS

Published by The History Press
An imprint of Arcadia Publishing
Charleston, SC
www.historypress.com

First published 2025

Manufactured in the United States

ISBN 9781467158268
Hardcover ISBN 9781540299970

Library of Congress Control Number: 2025941135

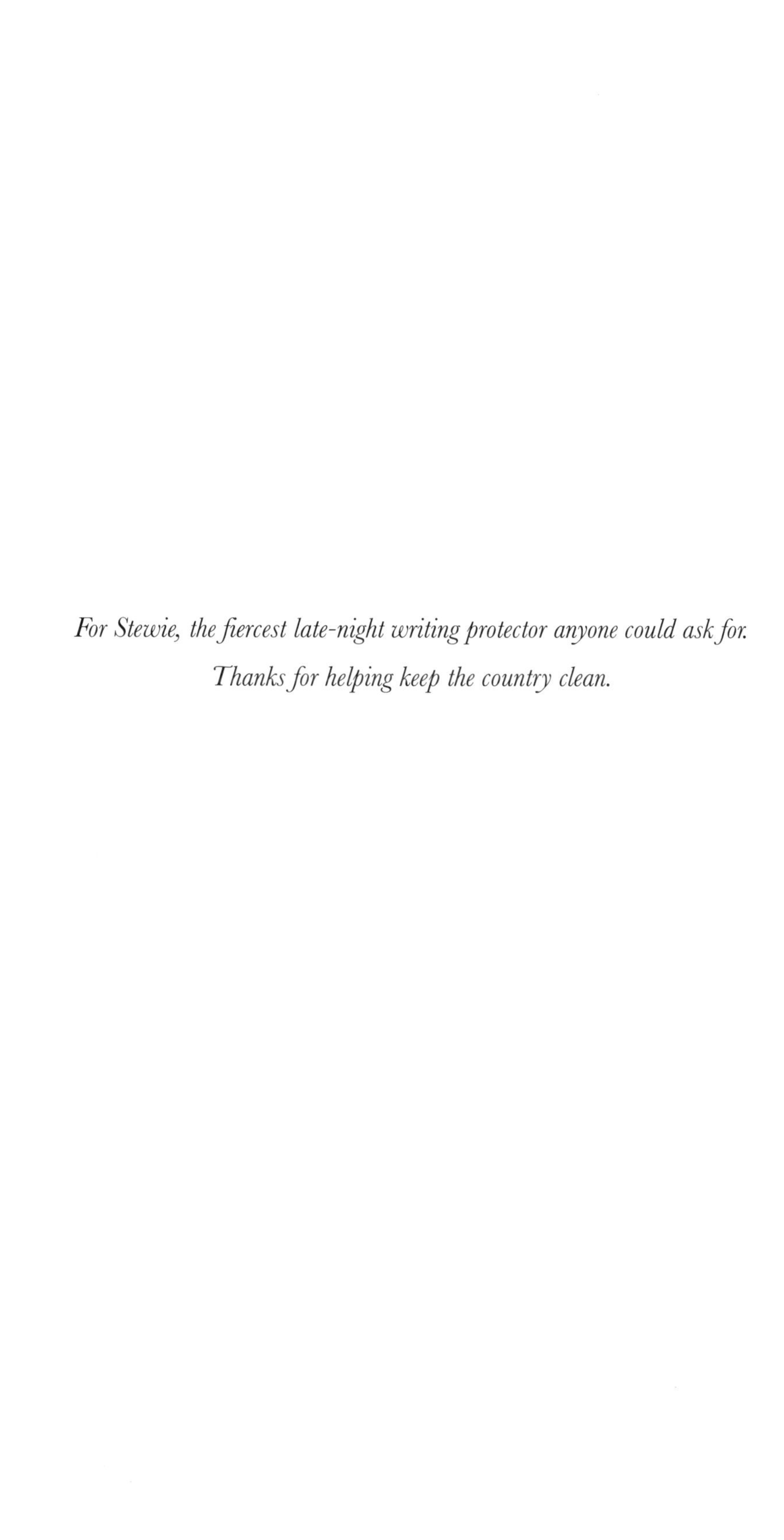

For Stewie, the fiercest late-night writing protector anyone could ask for.

Thanks for helping keep the country clean.

CONTENTS

Acknowledgements	7
Introduction	9
Part I. Ghostly Legends	
1. The Elmore Rider	13
2. The Haunted Steed	19
3. Ohio's Most Misunderstood Castle	24
4. The Bloody Bridge	30
Part II. Legendary Characters	
1. Snakes on a Grave	39
2. The Giants of Seville	46
3. Joc-O-Sot and the Cleveland Curse	54
Part III. Legendary Villains	
1. Jeffrey Dahmer's First Murder	63
2. Dillinger's Escape Plan	69
3. Pretty Boy Floyd	73
4. When the Satanic Panic Came to Northern Ohio	79

Contents

Part IV. Legendary Places
1. Deep Dive into the Blue Hole 87
2. The Lookout on Johnson's Island 90
3. Rogues Hollow 96
4. Buried Treasure on the Great Trail 100

Part V. The Unexplained
1. The Werewolves of Defiance 107
2. The Melonheads of Wisner Road 111
3. The Thing from Charles Mill Lake 116
4. Ol' Orange Eyes 120
5. Slithering Through Peninsula 125

Part VI. Legendary Events
1. The Ashtabula Train Disaster 133
2. Calling Michael Jackson 139
3. The Return of the Hinckley Buzzards 143
4. The Great UFO Chase of 1966 149

Selected Bibliography 155
About the Author 159

ACKNOWLEDGEMENTS

This book would not have been possible without the help and support of so many people, including the Chippewa-Rogues Hollow Historical Society; Jeff Craig; Hidden Ohio and Map in Black; Mikey and Bub at the Strange Road; Mark Delong; Samantha Nicholson; Sean Seckman; Wendy Cywinski, for not even hesitating when I asked her to take photos of cemetery sewers; Frank Yensel; Roger Ganley, the best strange and spooky roadie I could ask for; Sarah Marshall, Renee Hopper, and everyone at the Defiance Public Library; Oscar and his big beefy paw-paws; Brandi Hymer, for continuing to field my bizarre editorial questions; the late, great Richard Gill, for introducing me to the Elmore Rider; Scott and Forrest at Astonishing Legends; the Ghost of Jessica Graham; Patsy and Shema, for keeping me in line; Steve and Carol Flee; John Rodrigue at The History Press; Zoe Ames, for mad copyediting skills and being one of the few who actually gets my sense of humor; Chelsea Lundquist, my "work daughter"; and as always, Mark Moran and Mark Sceurman, for being the first ones to allow me to explore my weird side.

And once again, saving the best for last, none of this would have been possible without the love and support of Steph and Courtney, even if that meant waiting patiently in the car when things got too spooky or listening to my stories over and over again.

INTRODUCTION

What you are now holding in your hands is the final book in a series that has taken me all across Ohio in an attempt to chronicle some of my favorite legends and lore. Truth be told, when I was initially approached by The History Press back in 2016, I was only supposed to write one book: *Legends & Lore of Ohio*. I can remember responding, "That's not going to fit in just one book." After a brief pause, I heard, "Could you fit it in three books?" I agreed, even though I thought three books was still not going to be enough. I mean, if nothing else, I think I've proven to people that Ohio's a really weird state. Still, I agreed, because after all was said and done, I'd be able to act like a "real" author and say that I'd just completed my trilogy!

But what the size of this book—as well as the other two in the series, *Central Ohio Legends & Lore* and *Southern Ohio Legends & Lore*—forced me to do was focus. If I couldn't fit all my favorite stories in, I asked myself, which were the crème de la crème of Ohio's legends and lore? Not necessarily the most well-known or even the most popular—just the ones that stood out to me as the ones that prove, once and for all, that the Buckeye State knows how to bring the strange and spooky.

So what comes next for me, now that I've completed my trilogy? Well, with so many stories yet to be told, I can safely say you haven't heard the last of me. In the meantime, here's something you can do, even as a family, to hold you over: grab this book (or better yet, all three of the Ohio Legends & Lore books), throw it in your back seat and head on down the road to see some of these places for yourself. That's really what I'm hoping you get out of any book that I write. I'm hoping it moves you to want to experience the stories I'm telling. I've been writing about these weird things for decades, and still, nothing beats the rush of going my entire life not knowing something exists and then turning the corner and *bam*—it's right there in front of me. It's a thrill that can't be beat. I hope you get to experience it over and over again.

Ready for one last road trip with me? As always, I'll drive, and I've got plenty of snacks. Northern Ohio, here we come!

PART I

GHOSTLY LEGENDS

CHAPTER 1
THE ELMORE RIDER

I have often been quoted as saying that Ohio has more headless motorcycle ghosts per capita than any other state in the union. I have no idea why, but one thing is sure: the OG of them all is the Elmore Rider. However, pinpointing the origins of this story or even the exact location where this specter is said to appear is quite complex and can result in one believing one has lost one's head.

Over time, the legend has morphed many times, often changing its location. Suffice it to say, it has always been centered on the village of Elmore, Ohio. For the most part, the current version of the legend can be traced back to the 1940s. According to this version, things began around 1915 or 1916, when most of the world was engaged in World War I. But back home in Elmore, a local boy fell deeply in love. Locals reported often seeing the couple laughing and giggling as they rode through and around Elmore on the boy's motorcycle. Many believed that a date would be set for the couple to meet at the altar sooner rather than later.

Sadly, that date would never come to pass. In 1917, the United States entered World War I, and the young boy enlisted in the army and was almost immediately sent overseas. Before he left, the boy professed his undying love for the young woman, declaring that they would indeed marry upon his return.

Now, you're probably thinking you know where this story's going and that the boy never returned from the war. But as I mentioned, this story is full of twists and turns. When the war ended the following November, the boy was still alive and well, although it would still be a few months before he could return home. He finally returned to Elmore, Ohio, on March 21, and that's where the story really takes off.

Not wanting to waste a single moment, as soon as the boy was home, he threw down his bags, hopped on his motorcycle and took off to see his true love. When he got to her house, he could hardly contain himself and rushed inside, only to find the young woman in the arms of another man. Shocked with disbelief, the boy stood there a moment before stumbling back outside the house, blind with rage. He somehow managed to get back on his motorcycle, started it up and took off down the road at a very high rate of speed. Perhaps it was how fast he was driving or the tears of anger in his eyes (or a combination of both), but as the boy came to a bridge that crossed over a small creek, he lost control and crashed, decapitating himself in the process.

As you can imagine, the boy's death, along with the circumstances surrounding it, was something everyone in Elmore didn't like talking about. But then the whispers started about something strange happening out on the bridge where the boy died on March 21, the anniversary of the tragedy. People said they had gone out to the bridge and seen a white light, like that of a motorcycle, barreling down the road toward them, disappearing when it reached the bridge. Over the years, as more and more people visited the

One of several bridges said to have been part of the Elmore Rider's last ride. *Author photo.*

bridge, the story got tweaked a bit here and there (you now must flash your lights three times to make the motorcycle light appear), but the legend as it stands remains mainly unchanged: go to the bridge on March 21, and you will have the chance to see a ghost reenact a tragic event.

So is there any truth to the legend? More importantly, where is this bridge located? Well, beginning with the legend itself, while I have traced the current version back to the 1940s, I have found "ghost light" stories in Elmore, Ohio, going back to the 1920s. The strange thing is that before the 1940s, there was no mention of a motorcycle or, for that matter, any story explaining why "the Light" was there. It was described as a bright light that would appear in the middle of an unnamed bridge, flutter around and then move off the bridge to the west, where it would disappear inside an abandoned house, sometimes called the Spook House. There was no set date or time that you needed to be there to see the light.

Eventually, the Spook House took on a more prominent role in the legend. Sure, there were still versions of the legend that had the light starting on the bridge and disappearing into the house. But there were now newer versions where the light was said to be seen inside the house, and the bridge is never mentioned. It's these versions that give us the first explanation of who or what the light is: the spirit of a man who committed suicide inside the abandoned house. While the bridge doesn't play a significant role in these versions of the story, it was still a rallying point for people wanting to see the light: if they found the bridge, they just needed to look around to find the abandoned house where the ghost was. It would appear that once the house was demolished, the story refocused on the bridge. But which bridge and where?

Elmore, Ohio, is a relatively small village with a population of under 1,500 and very few bridges to choose from. Problems arise, however, if you take a fifteen-minute drive east of Elmore to Oak Harbor, Ohio. Wouldn't you know it? They have their own version of the ghost light, with a bridge and everything. These stories seem to have started in the 1920s, and while there may be a bit of legend-sharing between Oak Harbor and Elmore, a few specifics indicate that the Oak Harbor location is different from Elmore. For instance, the July 7, 1992 *Sandusky Star Journal* carried an article stating that the spook light was seen on Lindsey Road (the road, not a bridge), while the September 12, 1992 *Sandusky Register* claimed the light was located "five miles southwest of Oak Harbor near the Lindsey Road." Further confusing things is an article in the October 26, 1978 *News Herald*, which states, "Another ghostly tale from Ottawa county hangs by the 'ghost lights' that have been

Side view of the Elmore Bridge. *Author photo.*

seen along the Portage River west of Oak Harbor." Okay, so we clearly need to head back west, toward Elmore, to find the bridge.

As we take West Portage River South Road out of town, we're only about halfway to Elmore (still technically in Oak Harbor but very close to Harris Township) when we see a sign for Slemmer-Portage Road (a.k.a. Township Highway 43) coming up on our left. Taking that left, we travel a little over a mile down the road until we reach a small bridge that crosses Wolf Creek. This bridge is ground zero for the Elmore Rider ghost story as it stands today.

We know this to be true because, in 1966, a Toledo radio station did a live broadcast from Slemmer-Portage Road on Halloween Night, attempting to make contact with the "Elmore ghost." During the broadcast, they retold the same basic legend that exists today: a young boy returning from the war finds his true love in the arms of another man, crashes his motorcycle and loses his head. The only aspect missing from their version is that you can see the light only on March 21. Supposedly, hundreds of teenagers from local high schools got wind of the live broadcast and showed up on Slemmer-Portage Road, hoping to see the ghost. Everyone there, including the radio crew, left disappointed, as the ghost failed to show during the broadcast.

However, twenty years later, *News Herald* reporter Alesia Cooper managed to track down some of those teenagers who took part in the live broadcast and interviewed them, confirming that the bridge site was on Slemmer-Portage Road. Cooper even spoke with Vernon Bloom, who lived near Slemmer-Portage Road. Cooper remembered not only that the 1996 live broadcast was done from the road but also that the result was increased traffic through the area, including "cars from all over" parking on his property.

This is also the location that folklorist Richard Gill visited in an attempt to get to the bottom of the legend. Gill and an unnamed companion visited the bridge armed with audio and video equipment, intent on conducting a few experiments. They began by flashing their car headlights, not really expecting anything to happen. To their amazement, a mysterious light appeared in the middle of the road and started approaching them, disappearing just as it reached the bridge. The pair found that the light would appear each time they flashed their headlights, leading them to tie a string across the road to see if it would break the string as it went by. It didn't, which made Gill want to leave, but his friend wanted to try one last experiment: he wanted to stand in the middle of the road and see if the light would pass through him. Gill left his friend standing in the road and retreated to the car to flash the headlights. Almost immediately, the light appeared and made its way down

Did the Elmore Rider come racing down this hill to his doom? *Author photo.*

Left: Cover of the December 1972 *Journal of the Ohio Folklore Society*, which brought the legend of the Elmore Rider to all of Ohio. *Author photo.*

Right: Sweatshirt commemorating Elmore's legendary headless ghost. *Author's collection.*

the road toward his friend. When the light reached his friend, it disappeared, as did his friend. Gill jumped from the car and ran toward the spot in the road where his friend had been, finding nothing. A few moments later, Gill found his friend lying in the ditch alongside the road, semiconscious. Gill chronicled his experiences in the December 1972 issue of the *Journal of the Ohio Folklore Society*, which was distributed throughout Ohio colleges and universities, which helped spread the legend of the Elmore Rider to an even wider audience, spawning various other headless motorcycle ghosts along the way.

So what are we to make of all this? Is there really a headless ghost roaming the country roads just outside of Elmore, Ohio? I'm not convinced, but if you should find yourself driving along Slemmer-Portage Road, especially on March 21, and you should see signs for a bridge up ahead, keep a lookout. You never know who or what might appear in front of your car!

CHAPTER 2

THE HAUNTED STEED

I've always found merry-go-rounds and carousels to be both exhilarating and frightening. I love the idea that, in many cases, you are hopping onto history when you climb onto one of the carved characters. As the music begins to play and you start making your way around, waving to everyone you make eye contact with, you're hit with an overwhelming feeling of nostalgic joy. Yet carousel music always seems to be a little off, as if you're about to be transported to another time where things are not what they seem. Perhaps it's just the spinning creating illusions, but you almost start to think the horse you're on is getting ready to turn its head and look back at you. Or if you turn your head to either side, you might catch a glimpse of a ghostly woman riding on the horse next to you. Don't believe me? Well, visit the Merry-Go-Round Museum in Sandusky and see for yourself. After all, the museum is said to be home to a bona fide haunted carousel horse.

Charles W. Mueller, born in 1856, began his career as a general woodcarver. Whatever he carved, his clients appreciated his attention to detail and his ability to create incredibly intricate designs. He also enjoyed painting and often painted his carvings. Although it's unclear exactly when it happened, Mueller decided to merge his carving and painting skills, leading him to create carousel horses. His stunning, lifelike creations quickly became highly sought after, making Mueller a prominent figure in the emerging golden age of carousel artistry. What set Mueller apart from other carvers at the time was his unique way of capturing the essence of the carousel horse and bringing it to life. Rather than having his horses simply standing

Above: The haunted Military Horse, in all his glory. *Author photo.*

Opposite: The Military Horse is keeping his eye on you. *Author photo.*

there, Mueller designed them in striking, dynamic poses, which helped them look more lifelike when they were going around on the carousel. Mueller also utilized his carving and painting skills to make the horses' appearance convey a story, which made them even more lifelike. By the late nineteenth century, his works were highly sought after, and he became a leading figure in the world of carousel design. And of all the pieces he created for carousels, one of his most sought-after was his Military Steed.

The Military Steed, more commonly known as the Muller Military Horse, was a sight to behold. What set this horse apart was its unique military theme. Most carousel figures of the time were either mythical creatures or everyday animals. Muller's Military Horse was designed to reflect military pageantry, adorned with a military uniform and weapons. Overall, the horse inspired awe in all who gazed upon it. When it was placed on a carousel, it was not uncommon to see people racing each other to see who would be lucky enough to ride the horse. The horse became so popular that replicas were created and added to the carousel whenever the original needed restoration or just a break. The original horse has been on carousels or on display in Pennsylvania and Ohio, most notably at Cedar Point; it currently resides at the Merry-Go-Round Museum in Sandusky.

With such a storied history behind it, it should come as no surprise that the Muller Military Horse is said to be haunted. Like all good ghost stories, the one attached to the Muller Military Horse has mutated over the years. But the original version concerns a young woman who, on seeing the horse for the first time, immediately fell in love with it, so much so that she would stop at nothing to ride it, even if that meant coming back from the grave to do so.

Back when the horse was installed on the Cedar Point carousel, people would report seeing a ghostly woman sitting or standing alongside it. Ride operators sometimes saw a woman riding on the horse, only to find no one on it when the ride stopped. Other times, guests complained that they wanted to ride the Muller Horse but "some lady" wouldn't get off it. Every time the operator checked, no one was on the horse.

In some versions of the ghost woman legend, the ghost riding the horse is Mrs. Muller herself, who, like the other female ghost rider, loved this particular horse more than any of the others her husband created. In both versions of this tale, employees who shut the carousel down for the night report it mysteriously turning back on again and seeing a ghostly woman

Outside the Merry-Go-Round Museum in Sandusky. *Author photo.*

riding the Muller Horse, as if trying to squeeze in one more ride before the night ends.

Taking the horse off the carousel might have stopped the ghostly women from wanting to ride it, but they still show up and sometimes bring friends. When the Muller Military Horse was displayed at Cedar Point's Frontier Town, guests would report seeing men and women dressed in "period costumes" standing in front of the display that featured the Muller Horse. Most guests just assumed the costumed people were Cedar Point employees, even though no such employees exist.

Today, the Muller Military Horse stands inside the entrance to the Merry-Go-Round Museum in Sandusky, Ohio. And while I have investigated the museum several times in search of ghosts and have gotten some intriguing results, nothing related to the Muller Horse has ever occurred. That doesn't surprise me, though. I'm convinced that ghosts like to mess with me and purposely hide as soon as I arrive. Doesn't mean there aren't ghosts present; they just don't like hanging around me.

CHAPTER 3

OHIO'S MOST MISUNDERSTOOD CASTLE

Quietly looking down from a hillside in the North Chagrin Reservation of the Cleveland Metroparks in Willoughby, Ohio, is Squire's Castle, home to one of Northern Ohio's most enduring ghost stories. And while I dare anyone to show me a castle, anywhere in the world, that is not supposed to be haunted, the spirits swirling around Squire's Castle are undoubtedly unique, if for no other reason than the location of the haunting: the castle was never intended to be a castle at all. But first, let's look at the man responsible for the building's creation.

Feargus Bowden Squire was born near Exeter, England, in 1850 and migrated to the United States with his family around the age of ten. The Squires eventually settled in Northern Ohio. It didn't take long for people to notice that Feargus had a nose for business; before long, he was making a name for himself. In 1872, at the age of twenty-two, he cofounded an oil-refining company, Squire and Teagle. The following year, the company had become so profitable that it took on a new partner and was renamed Scofield, Squire and Teagle.

The money continued to pour in, and Feargus decided to retire from Scofield, Squire and Teagle and start a new oil-refining company, Newman, Squire & Co. Feargus really hit pay dirt when this company was sold to Standard Oil in 1876. Still, he chose to continue working at Standard Oil, serving as vice president and general manager until his retirement in 1909.

Around 1890, when Feargus was at the height of his success, he decided that he and his family needed a country retreat house. No doubt inspired

Entrance to the North Chagrin Reservation *Author photo.*

by the English country estates he had seen as a boy, Feargus envisioned a sprawling property, complete with several large brick-and-stone buildings. Of course, the centerpiece would be a massive, turreted castle-like main building. Before all that could become a reality, though, Feargus had to find a piece of property to build his estate.

Feargus eventually settled on land in the Chagrin Valley, roughly ten miles east of Cleveland. In all, he purchased 525 acres. Connecting with a New York architect, Feargus developed plans for two buildings on the property, the main building and a smaller building that would serve as the gatehouse and caretaker's quarters. It was decided that the gatehouse should be completed first as the main building would take quite a bit longer. Squire and his family could then live in the gatehouse while the main house was being constructed. Feargus officially named his estate River Farm.

Construction on the gatehouse began in 1895. Feargus decided to use locally quarried Euclid bluestone to create a castle-like appearance for the outer walls. The inner walls were constructed of brick and then covered in plaster and woodwork. When completed in 1897, the gatehouse featured several bedrooms across two upper floors, a main floor with a living room, a dining room, a kitchen with a walk-out porch and even a basement. However, it did not have running water, a sewer or natural gas.

After the gatehouse was completed, Feargus and his family often visited for weekend getaways. Construction continued on the property but mainly in the form of bridges, walls and miles of gravel roads. A large pond and a stream were dug—but no sign of anything resembling the giant castle locals had been waiting to see. There were whispers that Feargus was having issues finding building materials, hiring the right people or both. Still others hinted that Feargus had just grown weary of living in the country and wanted a sprawling mansion closer to the action in Cleveland. There may be some truth to the latter because, in 1902, Feargus announced the completion of construction on Cobblestone Garth, a Victorian mansion located along Wickliffe, Ohio's famous Millionaire's Row. Feargus and his family immediately began using Cobblestone Garth as their getaway destination, all but forsaking River Farm. Indeed, after 1902, it is unclear if any member of the Squire family set foot on the River Farm property. In 1910, the Squires moved into Cobblestone Garth full time.

As for the River Farm estate and the gatehouse, they were essentially abandoned and began to fall victim first to the elements and then to vandals. In 1922, Feargus Squire sold the property to a real estate syndicate. It, in turn, sold the property to the Cleveland Metropolitan Park Board in August 1925. The gatehouse continued to be heavily vandalized, often by late-night thrill seekers who had heard stories about the haunted building. Eventually, Metroparks decided that everything needed to be removed from the building for safety reasons: doors, windows, staircases and even the floorboards from the upper levels. The basement was even filled in with concrete. That is how the building stands today. Oh, and something else happened through the years: whenever someone asked about the building, locals would answer, "The Squire family used to live there." Keeping that in mind, when one looks at the remains of the gatehouse, it's easy to see how it came to be known as Squire's Castle.

So there's the history of the castle, which was never supposed to be a castle. However, the question remains: What motivated Feargus B. Squire to buy a large tract of land and invest a staggering amount in constructing what ended up being little more than a small outbuilding, only to walk away from the property without ever returning? We must look to the ghost stories connected to Squire's Castle to find an answer.

According to legend, Feargus's wife, Rebecca, was more of a city girl and didn't care for the whole country estate style of living. It was like an episode of *Green Acres* happening in Northern Ohio. In particular, Rebecca didn't like when her husband was called away on business. She was forced to spend nights alone in the old stone structure, surrounded by nothing by her husband's hunting trophies, whose heads were all mounted along the library's walls.

All that remains of Squire's Castle. *Author photo.*

As the story goes, Rebecca was alone in the upstairs bedroom one night when she heard a noise coming from downstairs. She took up a lantern and was making her way downstairs when she tripped, fell or was pushed down the stairs, breaking her neck. The next day, Feargus returned to the property and found his wife at the bottom of the stairs. It is said that Feargus came to believe that in the darkness, his wife was startled by one of his mounted animal heads, which is what caused her fatal fall. That, they say, is the real reason Feargus walked away from the Chagrin Valley, never to return: he couldn't bear to be reminded of his wife's tragic passing. Rebecca's ghost, however, apparently decided she wanted to hang around.

Legend has it that a strange red light, believed to come from the lantern carried by Rebecca Squire's ghost, can be seen moving back and forth across the windows of the second floor of Squire's Castle. The locals will tell you that it has to be a ghost: no living creature can walk on the second floor, since that was removed by the Metroparks decades ago. Sometimes, Rebecca's ghost ventures out of Squire's Castle and wanders the surrounding woods, still carrying a lantern. It's interesting to note that no one ever describes Rebecca's ghost, just the red glow of the lantern. Those who have tried to get a closer look have all reported that the lantern blinks out before they can see Rebecca.

Squire's Castle awaits your arrival. *Author photo.*

Another presence is said to haunt the castle, which is not as friendly. This entity is said to like to hang around the remains of the fireplace in the room many refer to as the Trophy Room. As this room was where Squire thought his wife saw something that startled her, causing her to fall, some believe that what inhabits this room is some nonhuman entity and that it was what Rebecca saw the night she died. Those who adhere to the story that Rebecca was pushed down the stairs will tell you that this entity also likes to hang out near where the staircases once were, including the one that would have led to the basement, waiting for another victim.

While the ghost stories surrounding Squire's Castle have endured for ages, two significant discrepancies immediately call the tales into question: Rebecca Squire did not exist, and Feargus Squire's wife didn't die at Squire's Castle.

Feargus Squire married Louisa Christiana Braymaier on December 26, 1876. They were still married at the time of Louisa's passing on October 29, 1927, roughly five years after Squire sold the Chagrin Valley property. Her cause of death is listed as pneumonia, and more importantly, Louisa's obituary states that she passed away "at her residence" in Wickliffe, Ohio, which is several miles from Squire's Castle's location in Willoughby Hills.

Still, we can't entirely write off the ghost stories surrounding Squire's Castle. Sure, the facts are that the person said to have died there didn't,

A shell of its former self, Squire's Castle still stands proud. *Author photo.*

and the structure wasn't abandoned due to tragic events, merely sold off when the owner appeared to get bored of the idea of living out there. But as I have said for many years, just because the ghost story is wrong doesn't mean the location isn't haunted. It could be a ghostly "chicken and egg" scenario involving ghostly activity around that property that had nothing to do with Squire's Castle. Perhaps, because we humans like everything tied up into a nice, neat little package with no loose ends, Squire's Castle got pulled into the ghost story to explain who the ghost was and why it chose to haunt the area. Am I on to something? Who knows, but this is where you come in. Take a ride out to Squire's Castle and see it for yourself. It is part of Cleveland Metroparks and open to the public. You can even wander around the wooded paths surrounding the castle. But you're on your own if you choose to tarry there after dark.

CHAPTER 4
THE BLOODY BRIDGE

You rarely come across an old bridge that doesn't have some ghost story or urban legend attached to it. Most attribute this to the idea that a bridge represents a crossing over or transition from one place to another. Still others maintain that bridges are symbolic of connections or communication. Either way, most ghost stories associated with bridges are incredibly vague. And then there's the case of the Bloody Bridge in St. Marys, Ohio. Not only is there a violent and bloody story associated with the bridge, complete with full names for all the principal characters, but there is also a historical plaque next to the bridge telling the complete story of the events leading up to the bridge's bloody name.

The giant stone plaque, placed there in 1976 by the Auglaize County Historical Society, chronicles the tragic events said to have taken place on the nearby bridge in 1854:

> *During the canal years of the 1850s a rivalry grew between Bill Jones and Jack Billings for the love of Minnie Warren. There became hatred by Bill because Minnie chose Jack. On a fall night in 1854, returning from a party, Minnie and Jack were surprised on the bridge by Bill, armed with an axe. With one swing, Bill severed Jack's head. Seeing this, Minnie screamed and fell into a watery grave. Bill disappeared, and when a skeleton was found years later in a nearby well, people asked was it suicide or justice.*

Historical plaque placed by the Auglaize County Historical Society. *Author photo.*

One could well imagine a tale such as this giving rise to the bridge being haunted—or several hauntings. Depending on which version you hear, the bridge is haunted by the headless spirit of Jack Billings and/or the murderous specter of Bill Jones. Some say that if you stand on the bridge and gaze into the water below, you might glimpse Minnie Warren's ghost floating below the water's surface. Of course, some claim the term "bloody bridge" is to be taken literally and that, after all these years, the bridge remains stained with Jack Billings's blood.

To determine if these ghosts are real, we must first unpack the ghost stories themselves. At first blush, the stories seem factual, as they include dates and the participants' full names. Perhaps most convincing of all, the county's historical society erected a sign about them. Still, we need to go back to when the story first began.

The earliest version of the story I could find in print is from 1894. The incredibly detailed article was picked up, verbatim, and printed in numerous newspapers across Ohio, including the *Cincinnati Enquirer* and the *Akron Evening Times*. The same story ran in Ohio newspapers throughout 1895; the last instance I could find was in the September 5, 1895 edition of the *Richwood Gazette*.

The story that everyone picked up and ran with begins with: "There is scarcely a person in Northwestern Ohio who has not heard of the 'Bloody Bridge,'" suggesting that the story was well-known before the article was first published in 1894. This tracks, as the events on the bridge are said to have occurred forty years earlier, in 1854. However, things get a bit cloudy toward the end of the article's opening paragraph, which states, "Few there are, however, who can recite the legend from which the bridge derived its ghastly name." So wait—everyone's heard of the Bloody Bridge, but hardly anyone knows how it got its name? This signifies that this 1894 article that made the rounds throughout Ohio for over a year is the starting point for the legend as we know it today. I say that because the article names all the main characters in the Bloody Bridge story and provides background information on them.

According to the article, Jack Billings and Bill Jones worked on boats that ran along the Miami-Erie Canal. The *Daisy* employed Jack, while Bill earned his pay on the *Minnie Warren*, named after the captain's daughter, who was also a cook on the boat. Both men were sweet on Minnie, but she loved Jack. As you can imagine, it made for an awkward situation when the two boats would pass each other on the canal and Jack and Minnie blew kisses to each other while Bill had to sit and watch.

Even the Ohio Department of Natural Resources calls it Bloody Bridge. *Author photo.*

Things came to a head (pun intended) in the fall of 1854, when both the *Daisy* and the *Minnie Warren* were docked for several days near the bridge while they were being loaded with lumber. Minnie and Jack received invitations to attend a party dubbed "the social event of that rural district." Bill Jones wasn't invited. By all accounts, the "frolic" was a huge success that went on until the wee hours of the morning. Jack and Minnie left the party arm in arm and were last seen heading toward the small wooden bridge crossing the Miami-Erie Canal.

On reaching the bridge, the couple were surprised to see Bill Jones standing there, holding an axe. According to the article, Bill exclaimed, "Ho! Ho! My pretty pair; you have played it fine to-night, but my turn comes now!" and swung the axe, completely severing Jack's head. Minnie "gave one wild shriek and swooned away, falling to the bridge's floor." Her "lifeless body" rolled to the edge of the bridge and then "went down to the watery grave below." People nearby, having heard Minnie's scream, came running to help, but by the time they got to the bridge, Bill Jones was long gone, and all they could do was pull Minnie's lifeless body from the canal. The story abruptly ends there without giving any information about what became of Minnie's and Jack's bodies or even where they were buried. As for Bill Jones, the article goes no further than to say he was never seen again, but it was believed that he drowned himself because, "years later," a skeleton was found in a nearby well.

With the legend out of the way, the article concluded with a few interesting tidbits, including that for forty years after the murder, Jack Billings's bloodstains were visible on the bridge, having "defied the rain and weather." However, the article states that "four years ago," a new bridge was built. The old one, complete with bloodstains, was broken into pieces, "becoming the property of relic hunters" who came from miles around to make off with "a piece of the blood-stained timber as a memento of one of the most horrible crimes ever committed." So while there might have been bloodstains at one point, they are long gone, and, as far as I can tell, what people refer to as "blood" on the Bloody Bridge is merely red-colored rust.

But the fact that the blood can't be tracked down and verified doesn't mean we can't still find historical documentation that the murders actually took place. I mean, we have people's full names, and a crime that heinous and well-known, at least at the time, should be easy enough to track down, right? Well, no. So far, I have been unable to find a Jack Billings, a Minnie Warren or a Bill Jones who lived or worked in that area during the time the events were alleged to have occurred. No newspaper reports of the murder,

This page: The Bloody Bridge, in all its glory. *Author photos.*

either. Which leads me to wonder: Where did the idea of erecting a plaque come from?

The answer lies in the August 30, 1961 edition of the *Delphos Courant*, which features an article by James Buchholtz. The article begins with a faithful retelling of the classic Bloody Bridge story. However, Buchholtz ends the article by stating that the canal is a "fast vanishing landmark in many sections," as are the many hamlets and villages that once lined it. But Buchholtz opines that "the legends of that old waterway, so closely linked with the history of our town, linger and, one suspects, will be recounted through untold generations." Inspired by that sentiment, the Auglaize County Historical Society placed the Bloody Bridge plaque near the bridge in 1976 to keep local history and folklore alive.

Of course, that does not explain the countless people who have reportedly had spectral encounters on and around the bridge for over 170 years. Are these the ghosts from a fateful and bloody encounter on the bridge? Or are they wandering spirits who chose to take up residence there? Even if they don't exist, one thing is sure: these ghosts and their stories have worked to ensure the area's history is not forgotten.

PART II

LEGENDARY CHARACTERS

CHAPTER 1

SNAKES ON A GRAVE

Imagine being so sure God doesn't exist that, on your deathbed, you give Him permission to fill your final resting place up with snakes. Well, if you believe the stories, that's precisely what one man, Chester Bedell, did in 1908. Moreover, it is said that after Bedell's passing, God took him up on his offer, and you can still see snakes wriggling around his grave.

Chester was born to Isaac and Cornelia Bedell in Sandystone Township, New Jersey, on December 6, 1826. Shortly before his tenth birthday, Chester and his family moved to Berlin Township, Ohio; his parents had been lured to Ohio by the promise of a better life. Of course, that meant living the pioneer life, as not much of Ohio had been developed. Living conditions were quite harsh for the Bedell family, even after they purchased a small tract of land and built a house, and Chester's educational opportunities were minimal. That didn't stop Chester, though. He loved reading and was always looking for ways to self-educate, including traveling to learn how others lived, worked and made money. One of the things Chester picked up on during his travels was how vital land and livestock were to all pioneers. With that in mind, Chester got involved in buying and selling livestock, and almost overnight, he became a leader in Ohio's budding livestock industry. Not content to stop there, Chester began buying up property across Mahoning County and reselling it at a profit. At one point, Chester Bedell owned almost 1,600 acres in the county.

On New Year's Day 1851, Chester Bedell married Mary Hartzell, a Mahoning County resident. The couple would remain married until Chester's

Chester Bedell's grave marker at Hartzell Cemetery. *Author photo.*

passing in 1908, and together, they would raise eight children. Still, according to Bedell's own account, this marriage was the root of all the snake stories. This was because his new wife was heavily involved with the local Presbyterian church. On the surface, that wasn't an issue, as Chester considered himself something of a self-taught biblical scholar. But he also fancied himself an atheist and started believing that congregation—and in particular, his father-in-law, Henry Hartzell—was perhaps trying a bit too hard to push their religious beliefs on him. Not one to sit idly by, Chester Bedell would take subtle jabs at the members of the congregation whenever he saw them out in public. Over the years, the jabs became less subtle, and it is said that Bedell would stand at the edge of his property on Sunday morning and mock the churchgoers as they passed by. In 1897, Bedell even committed his hatred to print by publishing his autobiography, *Twenty-One Battles Fought by Chester Bedell with Relations and Presbyterian Intolerance with a Short Sketch of His Life.* In it, Bedell chronicled his issues with his in-laws and with the Presbyterian church.

In the early 1900s, Chester Bedell, always the forward thinker, visited a local monument company and commissioned a solid bronze likeness of himself. Bedell wanted the statue placed over his grave on his passing. But this was to be no ordinary bronze statue: Chester gave precise instructions

Chester Bedell's monument, after his statue was removed. *Author photo.*

about the pose the statue was to strike. Bedell wanted his bronze likeness to stand tall, holding a scroll in his right hand that read, "Universal mental liberty." Under the statue's left foot, there was to be a book bearing the inscription "Superstition." When completed, the life-size statue matched Chester's description perfectly, and it's pretty likely Chester chuckled to himself when he thought of what everyone would think and say when it was placed over his family plot.

After a lengthy illness, Chester Bedell passed away on Tuesday, September 1, 1908. According to legend, as Chester lay dying, he was asked if he wished to confess his sins and ask God for forgiveness, to which he responded, "There is no God." Bedell allegedly took it even further by stating, "If there is a God, let snakes infest my grave." Very little, if any, historical documentation substantiates Chester Bedell ever saying these words, but they certainly play into how locals perceived him. As more proof of that, the local newspaper, *The Alliance Review*, announced his passing under the headline "Chester Bedell, Famed Infidel, Died Tuesday Night."

You would think this would be the end of the story, but it's not. Shortly after Chester Bedell was interred at Hartzell Cemetery and the life-size bronze statue was erected over his grave, locals began claiming to have seen a strange sight: snakes wriggling all over the grave. That brought more than a few curiosity seekers to the cemetery—and lo and behold, snakes were sometimes found at the grave. By and large, the snakes were dead and found draped over the statue of Chester Bedell, while the occasional live snake was found. Dead or alive, the fact that snakes could be seen over and around the grave of a man who supposedly dared God to put them there was enough to make people from all over the county come visit. Around this time, the theory was posited that perhaps all this snake business was the result of the local Presbyterian church trying to have the last laugh at Chester Bedell's expense.

A pattern started developing when it came to the best day and time to see the snakes on Chester's grave site. Wouldn't you know it? Your best chance of seeing the snakes was on Sunday before church. It seems members of the local Presbyterian congregation might have been going around and paying the local teens to catch snakes on Saturday night, haul them over to Hartzell Cemetery and dump them on Chester's grave. Those on their way to church Sunday morning would, hopefully, see the snakes on the grave and take it as confirmation that not only does God exist, but he also made a liar out of Chester Bedell.

The entrance to Hartzell Cemetery, final resting place of Chester Bedell. *Author photo.*

Above, left: Maybe those stories about snakes at Chester Bedell's grave were true, after all. *Author photo.*

Above, right: It's unknown who placed this particular rubber snake on Chester Bedell's monument. *Author photo.*

Left: Booklet that helped spread the legend of Bedell's grave being overrun with snakes. *Author's collection.*

Over the years, Chester Bedell's snake-filled grave grew into a tourist trap, including the usual souvenirs such as postcards. The back of every postcard featured a retelling of how Bedell dared God to send snakes his way. In 1956, a small thirty-eight-page book was added to the list of must-have souvenirs. Titled *The Infidel's Grave*, the book told the story of how Chester Bedell declared that if there was a God, He could put snakes in his grave. The book also included supposed first-person accounts of people who had visited the Bedell grave site and seen snakes.

Visitors to Hartzell Cemetery today may be disappointed to learn that the life-size bronze statue of Chester Bedell no longer stands over his grave site. However, contrary to the popular legend, which states that the statue was destroyed when God repeatedly threw lightning bolts down from Heaven, the statue still exists. It was removed from the grave site by members of the Bedell family and is currently on display, intact, at the Berlin Center Historical Society. Close inspection of the statue reveals what appear to be bullet holes, possibly a testament to the mortals who took issue with it.

As for the snakes, I've been to the cemetery numerous times and have yet to see a single snake, living or dead, at the Bedell plot or anywhere within the confines of Hartzell Cemetery. One time, my wife was startled by a rubber snake at the cemetery. When asked if I had put the snake there, I could neither confirm nor deny.

CHAPTER 2
THE GIANTS OF SEVILLE

When Martin Van Buren Bates was born in 1845 in Whitesburg, Kentucky, the only thing that could be considered "giant" about him was the size of his family. Martin was the youngest of eleven children. At birth, he was of standard length and size, but that would quickly change. By the time he entered his teen years, Martin was over six feet tall and weighed nearly three hundred pounds; no wonder he was given the nickname the Kentucky Giant around this time. Oddly enough, even after he was given that monicker, Martin still wasn't done growing—not even close.

In school, Martin came across as very bright and studious. After graduating, he enrolled at Emory & Henry College in Virginia, intending to study to become a schoolteacher. That goal would be put on hold shortly after Confederate troops opened fire on Fort Sumter in South Carolina, effectively starting the American Civil War. Feeling a kinship with the Confederacy, Martin withdrew from Emory & Henry and, in September 1861, enlisted in the Confederate army as a private in the Fifth Kentucky Infantry.

By all accounts, Martin was a courageous soldier, and he quickly rose to the rank of captain. Martin was so proud of this accomplishment that for the rest of his life, he'd refer to himself as Captain Bates and would often walk around in public in his Confederate uniform, much to the chagrin of his neighbors. Of course, during the Civil War, Martin used his size to his advantage, and rumors spread among Union troops about the "biggest rebel of them all," who was "as big as five men and fights like fifty." In essence, Martin became a boogeyman to the Union soldiers. However,

Martin's size had a downside: it made him an easy target. He was shot and severely wounded in Virginia during a battle near the Cumberland Gap. He was also captured and taken as a prisoner of war, although he would eventually manage to escape. But even while he was a prisoner, Martin could use his size to his advantage. While imprisoned at the Camp Chase Confederate stockade in Columbus, Ohio, Martin was given preferential treatment, and whenever Union guests came to Camp Chase, Martin's captors showed him off.

After the Civil War, Martin again used his size and appearance to his advantage when he joined the Robinson Circus and traveled throughout the United States and even parts of Europe. While he was initially billed as the "Biggest Rebel of Them All," his stage name was later shortened to Captain Bates. Regardless, he always wore his uniform when he was performing. Most of the time, Martin sat and let people look at him and then stood up to his full seven-foot, nine-inch height to gasps from the crowd. Other times, Martin read aloud from a book or told the audience about his travels. It certainly wasn't a strenuous gig, but the Robinson Circus traveled across the United States and Europe, which wore on Martin.

In 1870, Martin was traveling through Canada with the Robinson Circus when he heard stories about a woman from the P.T. Barnum Circus who was considered incredibly tall, even taller than Martin himself. Martin wondered why he hadn't seen this woman before and was told that while she worked for P.T. Barnum, she didn't like to travel with the circus. If Martin wanted to see her, he would have to go to the Barnum-owned American Museum in New York City. That's exactly what Martin did, and some would say it was love at first sight.

The woman Captain Martin fell in love with was born Anna Haining Swan in New Annan, Nova Scotia, in 1848. Like Martin, Anna came from a large family, one of thirteen children. Anna also had a huge growth spurt at an early age that lasted into her early twenties, when she reached her full seven-foot, eleven-inch height, a full two inches taller than Captain Bates. Even so, the captain was likely charmed by Anna's appearance and demeanor and how well known she was in New York society. For while Anna did not travel with P.T. Barnum, she would host afternoon teas at the museum and even at the homes of New York's movers and shakers. Anna was well cultured, spoke several languages and played the piano. Whatever it was, anyone who saw the pair together knew something special was forming between them. P.T. Barnum himself saw it, and that's when he devised a business proposition for the budding couple.

Barnum proposed that Anna and Martin go on tour together with the P.T. Barnum Circus. Barnum said crowds were always huge when it came to seeing the world's tallest person. There was no telling how immense the crowd would get to see the world's tallest couple. It could be a very lucrative business venture for all parties. It's unclear how much the potential to make money versus the chance to spend more time together played into Martin and Anna's decisions. Suffice it to say that Martin joined P.T. Barnum, and Anna agreed to go on tour. The pair set off for Europe in 1871, billed as the World's Tallest Couple, a designation they still hold today.

The couple's European tour was a wild success, resulting in a unique audience with Queen Victoria. The queen was so taken by the couple, Anna in particular, that that first audience was followed by several more. When Anna and Martin announced they were to be married, Queen Victoria pulled out all the stops, including insisting that she be permitted to commission Anna's wedding dress. On June 17, 1871, the couple was married at the historic St. Martin-in-the-Fields Church. Not only was the queen in attendance, but she also gave the newlywed couple several pieces of jewelry as wedding gifts. For the remainder of the couple's European tour, their billing was amended slightly: now they were known as the World's Tallest Married Couple.

On their return to the States at the end of the year, the couple decided it was time to settle down and start a family. They purchased property in Kentucky but found that the area was still reeling from the Civil War and the wounds were still relatively fresh. No doubt Captain Bates walking around town in his Confederate uniform didn't help things. By 1872, Bates was looking to sell his property and move out of Kentucky, telling friends, "I've seen enough bloodshed; I didn't want any more."

In late 1873, Martin and Anna Bates were excited to announce that Anna was pregnant with their first child. Given Anna's height and weight, complications were expected, and Anna did her best to take it easy in the months before the due date. On May 19, 1874, Anna gave birth to an eighteen-pound daughter. Tragically, the child was stillborn. Taking time to grieve, the couple decided to take a European trip and see their old friend Queen Victoria. While their previous European trips had been as part of the P.T. Barnum Circus, this time they went alone.

When the couple returned from Europe, they took some time to reconnect with the P.T. Barnum people they'd become friendly with over the years. One of them was animal trainer James Craven, who lived in Seville, Ohio. While they were in Seville, Martin and Anna liked everything they saw, mainly

Sign pointing the way to the Bates memorial at Mound Hill Cemetery. *Author photo.*

Grave marker for the "Giants of Seville" and their son. *Author photo.*

Above and opposite: The Bates family plot in Seville's Mound Hill Cemetery. *Author photos.*

the wide-open farmland. The excitement in town when everyone saw the world's tallest couple walking by clinched it, and Mr. and Mrs. Bates bought 130 acres of farmland in Seville. The world's tallest married couple had finally found their forever home.

But while they may have found their forever home, the house still needed to be built. Everything in the house was built with the world's tallest couple's comfort in mind, from the fourteen-foot ceilings and the eight-and-a-half-foot doorframes to the ten-foot-long bed and a basement dug deep enough that both Anna and Martin could stand in and walk through it comfortably. No expense was spared. They even had a giant, custom-built barn constructed, so big that it could easily hold all their carriages, buggies and sleighs, all custom-made to accommodate the couple's height and weight. One of the final touches on the property was to have "Captain M.V. Bates" emblazoned across the shingled roof, lest anyone wonder whose house it was.

From 1878 through 1880, the couple would go out on tour with the W.W. Cole Circus, but by and large, they stayed in Seville and became part of the community. Anna became a Sunday school teacher at the Seville Baptist Church, which she attended regularly with her husband, after a specially designed church pew was created for them to sit in. As for the captain, he took to the farming life and would often be seen in town, dressed in his Confederate uniform. Over the years, the road past the Bates property became a popular destination for people to take their carriages and buggies down, hoping to catch a glimpse of the Giants of Seville. If that didn't work, one could always head into town and look for them.

On January 18, 1879, Anna Bates gave birth to a son in what was described as a "difficult" birth. The boy was thirty inches long and weighed almost twenty-four pounds. In his autobiography, Martin described his son as "perfect in every respect" and said, "He looked at birth like an ordinary child of six months." Tragically, the child died only eleven hours after being born and without ever being given a proper name; he is merely listed as "infant boy." According to Guinness World Records, the child is considered the heaviest baby born in medical history.

Even though Anna had been experiencing health problems for some time, no doubt tied to her height and weight, it was still a shock to everyone when she passed away unexpectedly at her Seville home on August 5, 1888, just shy of her forty-second birthday. Grief-stricken, Martin commissioned a unique statue, to be created in Europe, to stand over the family plot he had purchased in Seville's Mound Hill Cemetery after the death of his son in 1879. The statue, which is now sometimes referred to as the Giant (even though that might have been in reference to the plot owner as opposed to the statue), is of a woman, standing tall and proud. Some say the statue was designed to look like Anna herself.

Martin remarried in 1900, to Annette Wetherby, the preacher's daughter, who was only five feet, four inches tall. What's more, Annette didn't want to live in the "Giants' House," so Martin put the house up for sale. The newlyweds purchased an existing home on the corner of East Main and East Streets in Seville. As this was a normal-sized house, Marvin had no use for all

Welcome to Seville, Ohio, home of the giants. *Author photo.*

his custom-built farming equipment and furniture. When it was announced that there would be a sale at the Captain's House, people came from miles around to take home something from the house as a souvenir.

Captain Marvin Bates passed away on January 7, 1919, at eighty-one. He is buried in the Bates family plot in Mound Hill Cemetery, alongside his wife and their infant son. After the funeral, Annette Wetherby sold off almost all the captain's material goods. Anything left of his estate was willed to Annette's family after her passing in 1940.

Even though the captain and his wife have been gone for over one hundred years, their memory lingers and can be felt throughout Seville. The couple is commemorated on historical markers throughout the city, and most recently, their likeness was added to the road signs welcoming visitors to "Seville, Ohio, Home of the Giants."

CHAPTER 3
JOC-O-SOT AND THE CLEVELAND CURSE

Ask any Cleveland sports fan, and they will tell you that no matter the sport, the team is cursed. But of all the teams, the one said to be the most cursed is the Cleveland Indians—er, Guardians. The curse is said to have been caused by one man, Chief Joc-O-Sot. And while there may be some truth to the events that may have caused Joc-O-Sot to enact a curse, the chief's storied history is often overlooked.

In 1810, Joc-O-Sot ("Walking Bear") was born into the Meskwaki tribe, a group of Native Americans that was part of the Sauk Nation. The Sauk resided in the Eastern Woodlands area of the United States, lands that now make up many of the Great Plains states. Several years before Joc-O-Sot's birth, in 1804, members of the Meskwaki tribe and the Sauk Nation signed the Treaty of St. Louis, part of which called for the Sauk Nation to give up ownership of all its land east of the Mississippi River. At the time of the signing, that land was almost entirely unsettled by pioneers—which, some say, is why the Meskwaki and the Sauk didn't think much about signing the treaty. Others would later claim that they didn't understand what they were signing. Either way, the ramifications of signing that treaty would take time to come to light.

Over the next few decades, settlers began pushing west. As they moved closer and closer to the Mississippi River, the people of the Sauk Nation found themselves being forced out. They went willingly at first, but it got to the point where they felt something needed to be done. Sauk Chief Black Hawk sent a message to the U.S. government declaring that the Treaty of

Joc-O-Sot, the Walking Bear. *N.d., lithograph, Smithsonian American Art Museum, Transfer from the National Museum of Natural History, Department of Ethnology, Smithsonian Institution, 1985.66.386,592AA.*

St. Louis was not a valid document as those who signed it didn't understand what they were signing and, in some cases, were intoxicated. Either way, the Sauk were not moving from their land.

In 1832, the United States responded by moving armed troops, led by General Edmund Gaines, into the area to intimidate the Sauk into moving west, over the Mississippi, as per the treaty. Black Hawk wanted to attack the U.S. troops and defend the Sauk's lands, but before he did, he consulted with Joc-O-Sot, who had risen to the rank of chief by this time. Joc-O-Sot agreed that what the United States was doing was wrong but believed that violence should never be the answer. After much discussion, Joc-O-Sot convinced Black Hawk to move over the Mississippi and wait things out. In doing so, Joc-O-Sot was able to stave off what he thought would be nothing short of a slaughter of the Sauk, as they were heavily outmanned and outgunned by the U.S. troops.

Unfortunately, Black Hawk only waited so long before he felt the need to react. On or around April 5, 1832, Black Hawk led a group of his men back over the Mississippi and declared that the land still belonged to the Sauk Nation. Still incredibly outnumbered, Black Hawk hoped for support from his allies, including Joc-O-Sot and even the British troops stationed to the north. When that didn't happen, Black Hawk approached the U.S. troops, attempting to call a truce. History is a bit cloudy about what exactly happened next, but the result was that someone in Black Hawk's entourage was "accidentally" killed. The result was the start of the Black Hawk War.

While Joc-O-Sot had hoped for a peaceful resolution, he was also wholly dedicated to protecting those in his tribe, so when the war began, he joined the fight. The Black Hawk War was short-lived: it lasted only fifteen weeks and ended in August 1832. Simply put, the Sauk were no match for the U.S. soldiers and militiamen. Joc-O-Sot himself was wounded during the war, and he would deal with the pain of that for the rest of his life. As part of their surrender, Black Hawk, Joc-O-Sot and the entire Sauk Nation were forced to admit that they no longer owned the lands and promise to vacate them, moving back west over the Mississippi River. This they did, but they left many natural resources, in addition to the land, behind them, and the tribe as a whole began to suffer. Seeing this, Chief Joc-O-Sot knew he had to do something.

After much thought, Joc-O-Sot decided he would cross back over the Mississippi River alone and look for work. If he found it, he would send what he could back to the Sauk Nation to help them survive. As he moved east, Joc-O-Sot initially found work as a trapper and a leader of hunting and fishing expeditions. Joc-O-Sot also found that many of his employers were fascinated by his stories about Native American life. All this came together when Joc-O-Sot made it to Cleveland, Ohio. There, he was befriended by Dr. Horace A. Ackley, the famous Ohio surgeon who would go on to found the Cleveland Medical College (now the medical school of Case Western Reserve University). Dr. Ackley was enthralled with Joc-O-Sot's stories and his proficiency with the bow and the tomahawk and came up with a way for Joc-O-Sot to make additional money. Dr. Ackley introduced Joc-O-Sot to Clevelander Dan Marble, a famous actor and comedian who was putting together a traveling vaudeville troupe. Joc-O-Sot was hired on the spot and began traveling with Marble's troupe. The troupe quickly gained a reputation as one of the area's "not to be missed" shows, meaning a grueling travel schedule soon developed for Joc-O-Sot as he traveled all over the Midwest, performing shows. The injury Joc-O-Sot sustained during the Black Hawk War sometimes made it hard for him to get around, but he was sending money back to help his tribe, so he kept pushing on.

Over the next decade, Chief Joc-O-Sot continued his travels, entertaining everyone wherever he went. The culmination came in March 1844, when Marble asked Joc-O-Sot to go to England and perform traveling shows with Irish composer William Vincent Wallace. In June the same year, Joc-O-Sot performed in front of Queen Victoria, who was so impressed that she commissioned a portrait of Joc-O-Sot. Sadly, it was on this trip that Joc-O-Sot became deathly ill. Initially, he believed it was just his old war wound acting up, but it is now thought he was suffering from tuberculosis or consumption. Whatever it was, it got to the point where Joc-O-Sot broke away from his European travels and returned to Cleveland alone.

Though he made it home safely, Joc-O-Sot became bedridden. It is said that he felt this might be his end, so he started asking people to return him to Sauk land so he could be buried there. His request was denied or ignored, and Chief Joc-O-Sot died in Cleveland on September 3, 1844. Shortly afterward, his body was taken to Cleveland's Erie Street Cemetery and buried there. This is when the ghost story and the rumors of a curse come into play.

It is said that since Jot-O-Sot couldn't get home and be buried among his people, his ghost is also unable to leave, trapped forever inside the Erie State Cemetery. They say that Joc-O-Sot's ghost rises from his grave at night and wanders around the cemetery, trying to escape. As dawn breaks, his frustrated ghost returns to his grave to try again the next night. If the legend is to be believed, Joc-O-Sot's ghost is so angry that it caused his grave marker

Right: One of the earlier stone markers placed over Joc-O-Sot's grave. *Author photo.*

Below: Chief Joc-O-Sot's final resting place inside Erie Street Cemetery. *Author photo.*

Opposite: Some believe Joc-O-Sot's spirit is responsible for breaking his tombstone. *Author photo.*

to break into the many pieces visitors can see today at the cemetery. And then there's the curse.

In 1994, the then Cleveland Indians opened their new baseball stadium, Jacobs Field, right across the street from the Erie Street Cemetery and Joc-O-Sot's grave. Soon after, rumors started making the rounds: Joc-O-Sot's ghost

Joc-O-Sot's grave lies in the shadow of the Cleveland Guardians' Progressive Field. *Author photo.*

was so angry that he decided if he couldn't be happy, "no other Indian" would be happy either. Essentially, he cursed the Cleveland organization, ensuring they would never be World Champions. There may or may not be any truth to the curse. Still, it must be pointed out that not even changing the stadium's name to Progressive Field or, more importantly, dropping the Indians name and renaming the team the Cleveland Guardians has changed the fact that the Cleveland baseball team currently holds the record for the longest active World Series drought: their last title was in 1948. Perhaps that's why visitors to the cemetery, especially on game days, often find Joc-O-Sot's grave site adorned with trinkets left behind by Cleveland fans trying to make peace with a ghost.

PART III

LEGENDARY VILLAINS

CHAPTER 1

JEFFREY DAHMER'S FIRST MURDER

When it comes to serial killers, few names evoke as much fear and outright repulsion as Jeffrey Dahmer, the "Milwaukee Cannibal," a man convicted of murdering close to twenty people. And while the vast majority of his crimes took place in Wisconsin, many are surprised to learn that Jeffrey Dahmer's murderous life of crime began in Northern Ohio.

Jeffrey Dahmer was born on May 21, 1960, in Milwaukee, Wisconsin, the first of two sons of Joyce and Lionel Dahmer. The family moved to Doylestown, Ohio, in October 1966, and in December that year, Jeffrey's brother was born. To show Jeffrey that he was an integral part of the Dahmer family, Joyce and Lionel allowed Jeffrey to choose his little brother's name; Jeffrey settled on David. By all accounts, the Dahmers seemed like any other family.

Things began to change shortly after the family moved to a home in Bath Township, Ohio, in 1968. The move marked the family's third in two years and Joyce and Lionel's sixth since their marriage. The house itself was lovely, surrounded by over an acre of woods. Experts have suggested that the frequent moves may have caused Jeffrey Dahmer's increased feelings of isolation and not fitting in. He had a few friends, but he mostly kept to himself outside of school, preferring to hang out in the woods near his house.

Sometime before his first year at Revere High School, Jeffrey started drinking alcohol. It started with beer but quickly progressed to hard liquor. He would drink during the day and be seen by fellow students drinking outside the school in the morning. Dahmer also concealed alcohol in his jacket and drank throughout the school day. He made a brief attempt to

Jeffrey Dahmer's 1978 senior photo from Revere High School. *Reverie 1978, original source unknown.*

fit in by joining the high school band, but by and large, he was considered a loner and an outcast. Oddly enough, despite his withdrawn and brooding appearance, Dahmer was considered a bit of a class clown, although that, too, had a dark edge to it. Dahmer was known to blurt out strange noises and pretend he was having a seizure, and he would do this in school as well as out in public. Eventually, so many people saw this odd behavior that it became known as "doing a Dahmer."

In early 1978, Lionel and Joyce Dahmer decided to divorce. While waiting for the divorce to be finalized, Lionel moved out of the house and into a motel. That spring, Joyce and David moved out of the family home to live with relatives in Wisconsin. Jeffrey Dahmer chose to stay in the family home, meaning he was all alone once again.

On the morning of Sunday, June 18, Dahmer was out driving in his father's car when he came across Steven Hicks, eighteen, who was hitchhiking alongside the road. Dahmer pulled over and asked Hicks where he was trying to go. Hicks responded that he was heading to Medina County's Chippewa Lake Park, which was holding its all-day Ohio Music Festival Appreciation Day. Dahmer said he would take Hicks to Chippewa Lake Park, but as it was still early, why didn't they swing by Dahmer's house for a couple of beers first? Hicks gladly accepted the invitation and got in the car.

The pair spent the next few hours at Dahmer's house, drinking beer, talking and listening to music. As the hour grew late, Hicks started to ask when they were going to leave for Chippewa Lake Park. Dahmer kept stalling, as he really didn't want to go to the concert. He wanted to keep hanging out in the house with Hicks. It felt like forever since Dahmer had heard a voice other than his own inside these walls. Eventually, Hicks must have given up on the idea of getting a ride to the concert and told Dahmer he was going to leave. Perhaps the fear of once again being alone caused something inside Dahmer to snap. He excused himself, went and retrieved a ten-pound dumbbell and struck Hicks in the back of the head with it twice. Hicks fell from his chair, unconscious, at which point Dahmer strangled him to death with the dumbbell bar.

Best bets

Christian rock group at Firestone tonight

Lamb, a Christian rock group featuring Rick Coghill (formerly of the Lemon Pipers) and Joel Chernoff, will be in concert at 8 tonight at the Firestone High School auditorium.

Tickets are $3 at the following outlets: Disc Records at Summit Mall, Berean Bookstores in Akron and Canton and Logos Bookstore in Kent. Tickets will be $4 at the door.

It's wall-to-wall bluegrass this weekend at the Fireman's Hall, 3975 Hametown Rd. in Norton. Bean Pole and the Blue Grass Mountaineers, the Greathouse Brothers and the Allen Coal Creek Co. are among the groups.

Music will continue all day today and from 10 a.m. to 6 p.m. Sunday. Tickets are $8 for both days or $4.50 for one. Parking is $1.

The Michael Stanley Band tops a list of six groups which will be performing Sunday at Ohio Music Festival Appreciation Day at Chippewa Lake Park in Medina County.

Breathless, Salem-Witchcraft, The Chris Michaels Band, Pegasus and Jim Ballard will be the other acts in this all-day stage show. The gates will open at 10 a.m.

Admission is $3 and tickets are available at all Ticketron outlets and will be available at the gate.

Chippewa Lake Park is off Ohio 224 near the I-71 truck stop.

Magic To Do, a musical collage of works from Godspell, Pippin and The Magic Show, is continuing at Weathervane Community Playhouse through July 9. Akronite Ernest Zulia is coauthor of the revue.

The play will be presented at 7:30 p.m. Wednesday through Saturday and at 8:30 p.m. Sundays.

Reservations may be made by calling the box office at 836-2626.

The film, "The Making of Ohio," which presents the story of the state's development through people like Benjamin Franklin Goodrich, the Wright Brothers and Mike Owens and Edward Libby, will be shown at 1:15 and 3:15 p.m. Sunday at the Summit County Historical Society, 550 Copley Rd.

The film runs 29 minutes and admission is free.

Announcement for the Chippewa Lake Park concert that Steven Hicks was heading to when he encountered Jeffrey Dahmer. *From* The Akron Beacon Journal, *Sunday, June 17, 1978.*

Dahmer would later say that he had not planned on killing Hicks and after he did, he panicked. He initially put Hicks's body in the crawlspace under the house, but he began to worry that his father, Lionel, might show up, looking for his car, and he would be found out. Dahmer knew he had to get rid of the body. But how?

After midnight, Dahmer went into the crawlspace and dismembered Hicks's body, placing the body parts in several plastic garbage bags. He then put the bags in his father's car and headed out, planning to discard the bags in random places across a wide area. While Dahmer was out on the road, a police officer noticed his car driving left of center. Given the late hour, the officer initiated a traffic stop to check the driver for possible DUI.

As the officer approached Dahmer, even though there was a dismembered body in his back seat, Dahmer was able to remain calm. Dahmer explained to the officer that his parents had recently divorced, and he was having trouble sleeping. He needed to take the garbage to the city dump, and since it was open twenty-four hours, he thought he might as well get it done now. The officer believed Dahmer, no doubt convinced by the garbage bags in the back seat, and after giving him a sobriety test, he let Dahmer go. Dahmer returned home and placed the body parts inside a drainage pipe on his property. He then burned all Steven Hicks's clothes and personal effects in a trash barrel.

Several weeks later, Dahmer took the body parts from the drainage pipe, broke up the bones with a sledgehammer and threw the pieces off the wooded, rocky cliff behind the house. By this time, Steven Hicks's family had officially reported him as a missing person, but there were no leads. The last anyone knew, he had left the Hicks's family home early on June 18, saying he was going to a concert at Chippewa Lake Park. Hicks's whereabouts would remain a mystery for the next thirteen years, until 1991, when they would be revealed by none other than Jeffrey Dahmer himself.

Fast-forward to the evening of July 22, 1991: Milwaukee police officers Rolf Mueller and Robert Rauth were on routine patrol when they were flagged down by thirty-two-year-old Tracy Edwards. Edwards frantically tried to tell the officers that he'd just escaped from the apartment of a guy he met at a bar. Edwards said the man handcuffed him and coldly remarked he was going to kill Edwards and eat his heart. At first, the officers weren't sure what to make of Edwards's story—until they saw the handcuffs hanging from his wrist. The officers asked Edwards if he would take them back to the apartment, and he agreed.

When the officers knocked on Jeffrey Dahmer's apartment door, they were confronted by the overpowering stench of what could only be described as rotting meat. The smell only got worse when Dahmer opened the door. He willingly allowed the two officers to enter the apartment, and from there, it didn't take long for them to realize that something was very, very wrong. Dahmer, who was detained as soon as the officers saw a knife sticking out from a mattress, remained strangely quiet and complacent, even as officers started finding human remains scattered throughout the apartment and the call went out for backup.

At the police station, Dahmer willingly confessed to the murders of multiple men and boys. There were so many victims that Dahmer's official confession lasted several days. Dahmer was charged with the murders of sixteen men and boys, but even after that, months of clarification meetings were held with Dahmer to try to—to put it bluntly—match up body parts and determine where all the body parts ended up. It was during one of those meetings that Dahmer mentioned a name the police weren't familiar with: Steven Hicks.

Not only were authorities working the case not familiar with the name, but Dahmer was also alleging the murder took place thirteen earlier in Ohio. Wisconsin authorities reached out to Ohio law enforcement and explained the situation. Ohio thought there was enough to go on and flew out to meet with Dahmer in person. During that meeting, Dahmer explained that evidence might still be found in the crawlspace, where he had dismembered the body. Dahmer wasn't sure if anyone would be able to find the bone fragments he scattered in the woods, but just in case, he offered to draw authorities a map.

In late summer 1991, armed with Jeffrey Dahmer's hand-drawn map, local and state authorities descended on the Dahmer family home in Ohio. It didn't take long for them to find evidence in the crawlspace, including a bloody handprint still visible on the wall. Locating the bone fragments was a more drawn-out process, and officials needed first to cut down the undergrowth and then begin sifting through the dirt, mostly by hand. Their tireless effort paid off, and on September 14, Ohio newspapers ran an interview with Summit County Coroner William Cox, who that stated the search of the woods had yielded 286 pieces of bone. Those fragments were confirmed as belonging to the body of eighteen-year-old Steven Hicks.

Jeffrey Dahmer was initially charged with the murder of sixteen men and boys. He was convicted of fifteen of the murders, and on February 17, 1992, he was sentenced to fifteen terms of life imprisonment plus seventy years. As

Dahmer guilty in Ohio murder

Associated Press

AKRON, Ohio — Jeffrey Dahmer, who confessed to the dismemberment slayings of 17 people, sat stolidly Friday as the mother of his first victim called him a "monster" and said she wished she could execute him.

"I will not be able to pull the switch on the electric chair, but if I could, I would on this animal," said Martha Hicks, the mother of 18-year-old Steven Hicks, who Dahmer has said was his first victim.

Dahmer pleaded guilty to a charge of aggravated murder in Hicks' June 18, 1978, beating death and dismemberment. A second count of aggravated murder stemming from the same slaying and a count of aggravated kidnapping were dismissed.

Jeffrey Dahmer pled guilty to murdering Steven Hicks. *From* The Cincinnati Post, *Saturday, May 2, 1992.*

for the Hicks murder, since it occurred in a different state and years before the others, Dahmer was charged separately for that. On May 2, he pled guilty to the beating death and dismemberment of Steven Hicks and was given an additional life sentence. All told, Jeffrey Dahmer killed seventeen men and boys between 1978 and 1991.

CHAPTER 2

DILLINGER'S ESCAPE PLAN

Throughout the annals of gangster history, one name tends to rise above them all: John Herbert Dillinger, the FBI's original Public Enemy No. 1. Rising to fame during the Great Depression, Dillinger became known for daring bank robberies and the fact that no jail could hold him. And wouldn't you know it: Dillinger's first jail escape happened in Lima, Ohio.

But let's start with the first and only jail Dillinger walked out of legally. On May 10, 1933, John Dillinger was paroled by the State of Indiana, having served nine and a half years of a two- to fourteen-year sentence for assault and battery with intent to rob and conspiracy to commit a felony. During his incarceration, Dillinger cozied up to many notorious criminals and gangsters. Now a free man with no means to support himself, Dillinger quickly returned to a life of crime, committing his first bank robbery in New Carlisle, Ohio, on June 21, 1933.

Dillinger's haul from the New Carlisle robbery was roughly $10,000. By all accounts, he was surprised by how easy it had been—so much so that he robbed another bank, in Bluffton, Ohio, on August 14. This one did not go as planned, and soon after, police were on his tail. On September 22, Dayton police finally caught up to Dillinger, and he was arrested and sent to the Allen County Jail in Lima, Ohio, to await trial for the Bluffton bank robbery. Oddly enough, when Dillinger was searched on arrival at the Allen County Jail, police found plans for a prison break on his person. Dillinger claimed he had no knowledge of a plan involving any prison break, so they shrugged it off. If only they'd known.

Four days later, on Tuesday, September 26, ten men, including several known associates of John Dillinger, escaped from the Indiana State Prison, using a method eerily similar to what was described in the paper found on Dillinger when he was booked at the Allen County Jail. In truth, it was no coincidence. While it was often called the Dillinger Escape Plan, the mastermind behind it was bank robber Harry "Pete" Pierpont. Pierpont, who was serving ten to twenty-one years for bank robbery, had made friends with other bank robbers, and they would often pass the time planning out the different ways they could break out. While Dillinger was incarcerated there, he joined the group of schemers. To a man, they all agreed that if an escape was going to be successful, guns would be needed. And when Dillinger was the first of the gang to get paroled, it was decided that he would be the one to figure out a way to smuggle guns into the prison. It's never been proven with 100 percent certainty how he did it, but everyone agrees that the firearms used during the Indiana State Prison break came from Dillinger. Knowing this now, it seems odd that more thought wasn't given to the possibility that some of those escapees might be heading to Lima, Ohio, to return the favor and bust Dillinger out.

John Dillinger's mug shot. *FBI Repository, original source unknown.*

OHIO SHERIFF SLAIN, BANK BANDIT FREED

Gunmen Friends of John Dillinger Shoot Official and Flee From Lima After Liberating Him

The news of Dillinger's escape from the Lima jail spread quickly. *From* The Daily Capital News, *Friday, October 13, 1933.*

On October 12, Harry Pierpont and two of the other prisoners who had escaped the Indiana State Prison, Russell Clark and Charles Makley, showed up at the Allen County Jail, claiming they were from the Indiana State Prison and had come to retrieve John Dillinger and return him to prison for violating his parole. Sheriff Jeff Sarber, who was alone in the jail, seemed skeptical and asked the three men for their credentials. At this point, Pierpont exclaimed, "Here's our credentials!" and shot Sarber. Sarber's wife, Jess, and Deputy Wilbur Sharp heard the gunshot and came into the jail to find the three men beating the sheriff, demanding the keys to Dillinger's cell.

The sheriff refused to turn over the keys, so the beatings continued until Lucy Sarber retrieved the keys from a desk drawer so that the men would stop beating her husband. Once they got Dillinger out of his cell, they locked Lucy Sarber and Deputy Sharp inside it. The men then took every gun they could find in the jail, including Sheriff Sarber's personal revolver. Leaving the sheriff bleeding on the jail floor, the group fled the jail and went on the run. Sheriff Jeff Sarber succumbed to his injuries shortly thereafter. While no one alleged that Dillinger himself pulled the trigger or was involved in the beating of the sheriff, the fact that his name was mentioned in the same sentence as "sheriff murdered" only served to make John Dillinger a bigger target for law enforcement.

Dillinger, Pierpont, Clark and Makley skirted law enforcement for the remainder of 1933, moving throughout the United States. Of course, they needed money for all that traveling, so the group pulled off the occasional bank robbery. The new year saw the gang heading west, eventually ending up in Tucson, Arizona. The plan was to lay low with the money they had acquired through several recent bank robberies. But those wads of cash would lead to all four men being recognized and arrested on January 25, 1934. When he was arrested, Pierpont was found to have Sheriff Sarber's personal Colt revolver. Based on that, as well as eyewitness testimony from both Lucy Sarber and Deputy Sharp, Pierpont, Clark and Makley were shipped back to Ohio to stand trial for the murder of Sheriff Sarber. Dillinger, on the other hand, was wanted in connection with the slaying of Officer William O'Malley, which had occurred during the robbery of the First National Bank in East Chicago, Indiana, and he was extradited to Indiana.

Not wanting a repeat of the jailbreak in Lima, police decided to house Dillinger at the Lake County Jail in Crown Point, Indiana, as it was deemed escape-proof. To be safe, additional guards were posted throughout the facility. None of that mattered, though, because on Saturday, March 3, Dillinger pulled out a pistol during morning exercises and was able to escape with fifteen other inmates, all without firing a single shot. While Dillinger certainly left the jail with egg on its collective face, the FBI file on the incident make matters worse by stating that Dillinger's gun was fake and that he carved it himself from shelving in his cell. This led to FBI Director J. Edgar Hoover officially naming John Dillinger the first Public Enemy No. 1 in late April 1934.

John Dillinger would never have the opportunity to escape from another prison. Just three short months after topping the public enemy list, on July 22, 1934, he was gunned down by federal agents outside the Biograph

An exhibit at the Allen County Museum features artifacts and a life-size re-creation of Dillinger's escape. *Author photo.*

Theater in Chicago. Over the course of the year after Dillinger was released from prison (in June 1933) until his death, it is estimated that he participated in over a dozen bank robberies. He was also imprisoned several times and managed to escape from the last two, including the Allen County Jail in Lima, Ohio—which, some say, marked the beginning of the end for him.

CHAPTER 3
PRETTY BOY FLOYD

Front-page headlines from newspapers across the United States all screamed the news on July 22, 1934: John Dillinger, Public Enemy No. 1, was dead, gunned down by members of the Bureau of Investigation (BOI) outside a Chicago theater. With Dillinger gone, the BOI needed a new Public Enemy No. 1, and the announcement was made the following day. The new Public Enemy No. 1 was Pretty Boy Floyd.

It wasn't as if seeing Pretty Boy Floyd at the top of a most wanted list surprised anyone in law enforcement. Long before the Pretty Boy monicker was born, Charles Arthur Floyd was known to authorities. He first came to their attention when, in 1929, at eighteen, he walked into the post office in his hometown of Akins, Oklahoma, and stole $3.50. This was Floyd's introduction to the U.S. legal system, one with which he became all too familiar through a series of bank robberies, murders and even an escape from the Ohio State Penitentiary. All of this was certainly enough to put Pretty Boy Floyd on the list, but it was his alleged involvement in the Kansas City Massacre that put him over the top.

On June 17, 1933, federal prisoner Frank "Jelly" Nash was being escorted by law enforcement and federal agents back to the U.S. Penitentiary at Leavenworth, Kansas. The journey began via train, which was to pull into the Union Station Railroad Depot in Kansas City, Missouri, where the group would quickly get into unmarked cars waiting outside the depot. The group arrived at the station without incident. But as they made their way to the waiting vehicles, they were ambushed by several men, who began firing indiscriminately into the group. The gunshots rang out for almost thirty seconds. When all was said and done, four members of law enforcement were dead, as was Frank Nash. Authorities quickly interviewed witnesses in an attempt to identify the shooters. The first man to be positively identified as a shooter was Adam "Eddie" Richetti. As Richetti was known to hang out and commit crimes with Pretty Boy Floyd, it wasn't long before Floyd was IDed as a shooter, although some now believe he was not involved. Either way, both Floyd and Richetti were officially listed as suspects wanted in connection with the June 17 shooting, now referred to as the Kansas City Massacre, and the pair had been on the run ever since word got out that they were wanted men.

In October 1934, Floyd and Richetti, who were holed up in Buffalo, New York, decided to head west. Loading up a car with guns, ammo and two female companions, they left Buffalo under the cover of darkness on October 18. Around three o'clock in the morning on October 19, they had crossed into Ohio and were traveling west when they encountered heavy fog. The car hit a telephone pole and slid off the road into a cornfield. No one was seriously injured, but the car wouldn't start. Floyd and Richetti sent their companions back toward the closest town in search of a tow truck to come out and pick up the car. Not wanting to be recognized, the two chose to stay with the vehicle.

Shortly after dawn on October 19, Joe Fryman was driving through the area with his son-in-law, David O'Hanlon, when the pair witnessed a strange sight not generally seen on the back roads of rural Ohio: two men dressed in suits lying alongside the road. It was as if the well-dressed men were trying to hide from someone. That raised Joe Fryman's suspicions enough for him to drive into Wellsville, Ohio, and report what he had seen to Police Chief John H. Fultz. The chief agreed that something seemed odd and decided to drive out and investigate. He asked Officers Grover Potts and William Erwin to accompany him.

As Fultz and his officers approached the scene, they didn't see anything at first, as Floyd and Richetti were still hiding. But as the patrol cars came to a stop, Richetti popped up from his hiding spot and began running toward the nearby woods. Almost immediately afterward, Floyd began firing at the officers, wounding Fultz and Potts. Floyd then fled into the woods, in the opposite direction from Richetti. Fultz and his men decided to follow Richetti, and they were able to apprehend him. Floyd, however, remained at large.

News of Pretty Boy Floyd's involvement in another shootout, this time in Northern Ohio, spread quickly, eventually reaching BOI Special Agent in Charge Melvin Purvis, who had been involved with the John Dillinger capture. When Purvis got word of the shootout with Floyd and Richetti and that Floyd was still on the lam, he was in Cincinnati with his team of agents, working on a kidnapping case. Purvis requested and received permission to leave Cincinnati and head to Northern Ohio to see if he and his men could track down Floyd.

On October 22, Floyd, who had been keeping himself hidden since the shootout with authorities, found himself on the doorstep of Ellen Conkle, a widow who lived in a farmhouse in East Liverpool, Ohio. Seeing that Conkle didn't recognize him, Floyd told her he had been drunk and was trying to return home. He also asked Conkle if she had anything to eat. Conkle later told reporters she did not know who Pretty Boy Floyd was and described the stranger on her doorstep as a "very pleasant man." She also said she served Floyd a meal consisting of spare ribs, potatoes, rice, pumpkin pie and coffee, for which he insisted she take a dollar, since it was a meal "fit for a king."

After the meal, Floyd read the local newspaper and asked Conkle if she knew anyone with a car who could drive him "out to the highway" (now Ohio State Route 7). Conkle remarked that her brother, Stuart Dikes, was out in the fields with his wife and that they had a car parked behind the corncrib. Conkle said they would happily take Floyd where he wanted to go.

What happened next is something that continues to be debated today. But according to what Ellen Conkle told reporters that afternoon, she watched Floyd walk with her brother and sister-in-law to their car, which was partially obscured behind the corncrib. All three got into the car; her brother, Stuart Dikes, was driving. As the vehicle backed out from behind the corncrib, Conkle said, two cars started coming down the lane toward the corncrib. In one car was Melvin Purvis and three of his agents. In the other was East Liverpool Police Chief Hugh McDermott and three of his officers. Floyd saw the cars approaching, and Conkle said she heard him yell from the vehicle, "Drive back behind the crib, quick. They are after me!"

Her brother reversed the car back behind the corncrib, Conkle said, and she heard Floyd yell for everyone to run. Then she saw Floyd jump from the car and start running across the field. Conkle would tell reporters:

> *The Federal men jumped out of their car and ran after him. As they passed my brother, they asked him who the man was and my brother replied he did not know. So they started shooting.*

The front of the Ohio Historical Marker near the site where Pretty Boy Floyd died. *Author photo.*

Conkle's statement that the agents fired first is in direct conflict with the BOI report on the incident, which states that when Floyd emerged from the car, he brandished a .45 caliber pistol and began firing at the agents, forcing them to return fire. Conkle did mention that Floyd indeed shot "a couple of times at them [the agents], but I don't think he hit anybody." Floyd wasn't so lucky: after running about two hundred feet across the field, he fell to the ground, having been shot.

Once again, there are several different versions of what happened next. According to the BOI account, which also claims Purvis and his men were the only ones on the scene (even though Conkle specifically said there were two cars), Purvis ordered Floyd to halt. When he refused, Purvis gave the order to open fire on Floyd. Purvis stated that he was the one who got to Floyd first, handcuffed him and then tried to interrogate him, but Floyd died on the spot. Many years later, a retired member of the East Liverpool Police Department would come forward to say not only that the East Liverpool police were there on the scene but also that *he* was the one who shot Floyd—albeit purposely in the leg so as not to kill him, just to stop him from continuing to flee. Purvis then walked up to where Floyd lay injured and ordered one of his agents to shoot Floyd at point-blank range. Still another

The back of the Ohio Historical Marker, riddled with bullet holes. *Author photo.*

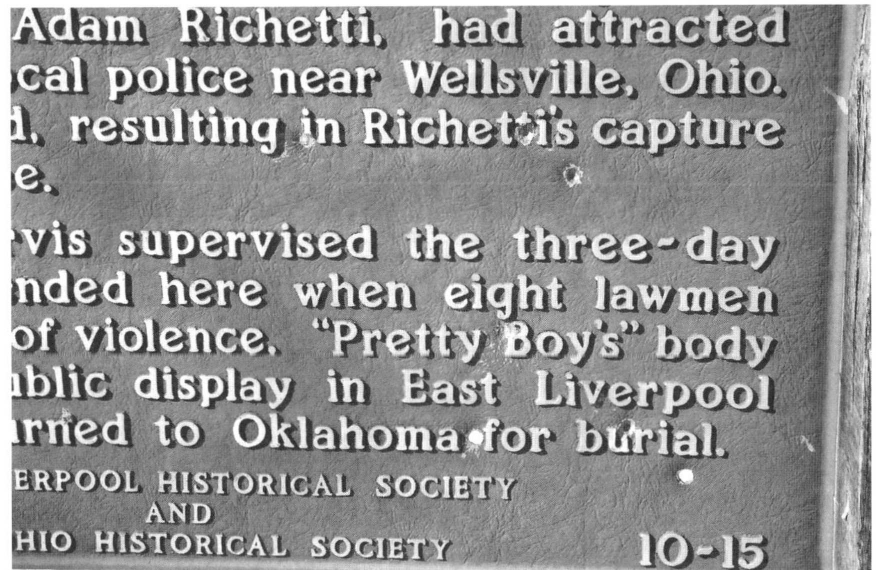

Close-up of the bullet holes that dot Pretty Boy Floyd's historical marker. *Author photo.*

version was given by Agent Winfred Hopton, who was on the scene that day. According to Hopton, while East Liverpool police officers were there, they did not arrive until after Floyd had been shot. As for the agents, they were merely returning fire from Floyd.

The only thing all accounts agree on is that Pretty Boy Floyd died in Ellen Conkle's field on October 22, 1934, as the result of multiple gunshot wounds. Floyd's body was taken to the Sturgis Funeral Home in East Liverpool, Ohio, where it was embalmed in preparation for being shipped back to Floyd's home state of Oklahoma. The funeral home also attempted to hold a public viewing of Floyd's body, but so many people showed up that the funeral home was overrun and had to close. For this reason, since Floyd's hometown of Akins, Oklahoma, was tiny (fewer than three hundred people lived there), the decision was made to hold his funeral in the larger town of Sallisaw, Oklahoma, a short distance away. It is estimated that well over twenty thousand people attended Pretty Boy Floyd's funeral, which still stands as the largest funeral in Oklahoma history. Floyd was then buried in Akins Cemetery.

After the funeral, there was a public outcry against the BOI, primarily directed at Special Agent in Charge Melvin Purvis. At the time, gangsters were looked at as something of folk heroes, and here was another case of Purvis being on the scene of a fatal gun battle with a gangster (first Dillinger and then Floyd). J. Edgar Hoover, director of the BOI, had always let Purvis do things his way, as that got results. But after the Floyd incident, Hoover switched gears and tightened his leash on Purvis. Some say it was because Hoover felt intimidated by all the publicity Purvis was getting. Either way, Purvis was having none of it, and he resigned in 1935, not even a year after Floyd's death.

Many of the things associated with Pretty Boy Floyd's last hours are long gone, including most of the Conkle farm. But in 1993, the Ohio Historical Society and the East Liverpool Historical Society placed a historical marker near the site where Floyd was shot and killed. Of course, the plaque is riddled with bullet holes.

CHAPTER 3

WHEN THE SATANIC PANIC CAME TO NORTHERN OHIO

As someone who spent his formative years during the Satanic Panic of the 1980s, I can honestly say I never understood what all the fuss was about. Having grown up with three older sisters, I was already well acquainted with the idea that every generation has something parents freak out over, worrying that whatever it is will get their children. Didn't matter if it was drugs or communism; it was coming for your children, and if you wanted to be a good parent, you needed to be on the lookout for the warning signs. Don't even get me started on popular music, because the idea that teenagers sometimes listen to certain music to tick their parents off is as old as time. But something happened in the 1980s: a wave of fearing what we don't understand rose and turned into the notion that secret satanic cults were sweeping across the nation and corrupting our youth through movies and music, right under our noses. Before long, mass confusion and unsubstantiated claims became the norm. Perhaps nowhere was this more evident than in Northern Ohio in June 1985, when authorities were digging up empty fields for evidence of satanic cult activity.

It all began on the morning of Thursday, June 20, 1985, when police raided a house on Crissey Road in rural Springfield Township, Ohio. The house belonged to fifty-nine-year-old Leroy Freeman, who was a suspect in the disappearance of his granddaughter, Charity. Neither had been seen in over two years, and the public was initially told that authorities were hoping to find Freeman and/or his granddaughter inside the house. Barring that, perhaps they could find some clues to their whereabouts or what might have happened to them. It made sense—until the sheriff decided to hold a press conference and discuss what they were really looking for.

Shortly after the raid, Lucas County Sheriff James Telb told reporters that the raid was the first step in an investigation that had begun three months earlier. Sheriff Telb said that a female informant had provided his office with information indicating that a satanic cult had been operating in the area for some time and that she had personally seen children being sacrificed during rituals in nearby woods and fields. What's more, the informant said she believed Leroy Freeman was the leader of the satanic cult and his granddaughter may have been one of the cult's victims. That was the real reason they chose to raid Freeman's home, even though he hadn't been seen there in over two years. Sheriff Telb continued by saying that authorities had removed items from the house that could substantiate the claim that the house had been used for cult activity. Then came the big bombshell: Telb said the raid had been only the first step in the investigation and the next one would occur later that day. Work crews were heading to nearby woods to begin digging, searching for what the informant told police would be the bodies of between fifty and sixty people, all of whom had been sacrificed by the cult and buried there. The sheriff said that the cult had allegedly been burying bodies there for the better part of sixteen years. Telb ended the press conference by saying he would keep everyone abreast of what was happening and hold future press conferences as needed.

Reporters scrambled in every direction as soon as he was done talking. Some went after the earthmovers they had just seen rumble past the press conference, no doubt heading to the dig site. Others went to try to get ahold of the official search warrant for the Crissey Road house to see exactly what was on it. Still others went off to try to talk to the current residents of the Crissey Road house and get the inside scoop on what happened during the raid.

The search warrant was rather vague, but it was clear that its primary purpose was to see if there was any evidence of Leroy Freeman or his granddaughter in the house. On the list of specific things to be on the lookout for, there were the usual "guns" and "drugs," but one line item stuck out from all the others: "cult paraphernalia."

At the Crissey Road house, reporters spoke with Patricia Litton, who lived there with her husband, Alvin, and their five children. Patricia, who was home with all five children at the time of the raid (Alvin was at work), said the sheriff's deputies showed up unannounced; forced her and her children to remain in one room during the entirety of the search, which lasted over two and a half hours; and essentially ransacked the house, throwing the contents of closets, dressers and cabinets on the floor. When asked about any cult paraphernalia, Patricia showed reporters a list of items that were confiscated, which included a bone, two Ozzy Osbourne records, a *Raiders of the Lost Ark* movie poster, two blank tapes and a Bible. Patricia also said the sheriffs wanted to seize the goat she kept in the backyard. They allowed her to keep it only after she convinced them it was merely a pet.

That afternoon, less than a mile from Crissey Road, digging began in a remote forty acres of woods. In addition to the police presence, Sheriff Telb had brought in several experts to help oversee the dig, including archaeologist G. Michael Pratt and Captain Dale Griffis, an occult expert from the Tiffin Police Department. At the end of the day, having unearthed nothing more than a rusty knife, a headless plastic doll and a hypodermic needle, Sheriff Telb said he was suspending the dig for the evening but that they would pick it back up tomorrow. These things take time, Telb said. And since this cult was rumored to have up to two hundred members, there was no telling how much evidence they'd be able to collect once they started digging in the right spot.

On Friday, June 21, authorities announced they would be focusing on two specific areas, which they had reason to believe contained the bodies of at least four cult victims. Authorities remained confident as cult expert Dale Griffis pointed out a mound of fresh dirt and sand surrounded by a rusty fence and suggested they dig there. Their confidence began to fade, though, when the dig revealed nothing and the mound of dirt and sand was determined to be nothing more than "back dirt from a groundhog hole." At the end of the day, Sheriff James Telb announced that he was calling off the dig, stating he had information that suggested his informant "may have been perpetrating a hoax." The great Satanic Cult Dig was over, or so everyone thought.

On July 2, digging resumed. Sheriff Telb claimed he had received new information and that this time, they would recover the bodies of cult victims. But by now, residents and even township board members had had enough, and the public outcry was immediate. D. Hilarion Smith, chairman of the township board of trustees, went so far as to call the allegations of human sacrifices and satanic rituals "crazy" and demanded Sheriff Telb stop immediately. Smith even mentioned that he and the sheriff had butted heads during the first digs when he gave the sheriff an ultimatum: find your first body within twenty-four hours or pack up and get out. For this dig, people were demanding Telb name his informants or, at the very least, explain why

B-4 METRO THE CINCINNATI ENQUIRER Tuesday, July 16, 1985

Investigators Backing Away From Death Cult Accusations

BY SUE CROSS
The Associated Press

TOLEDO, Ohio—Deputies have put back the Spencer Township soil they sifted for human bones. They have packed up so-called proof of a satanic cult. And talk in the rural township has turned to the weather— not the whereabouts of devil-worshippers.

The witch hunt has ended, at least in the minds of local residents who still question whether tales that sent Lucas County Sheriff James Telb on a futile search for supposed human sacrifice victims last month were part of an elaborate hoax, a case of misplaced heroics or a legitimate investigation.

The invasion of Spencer Township by reporters and law officers began June 20, when Telb told reporters he was digging in the wooded area about 15 miles west of Toledo for remains of 50-75 human victims of occult ceremonies. He said informants told him the cult's 200 members had been sacrificing some five people a year since 1969.

Three days of digging found no sign of human remains, and the sheriff who said then that "there is no question about the cult operating here," is taking a more tentative stance.

"If in fact there is a cult—and I say 'if'—it involves a lot of people," Telb told residents last week at a township meeting where he came to defend his investigation.

"We've always said if our information is correct—if, if, if."

Deputies did find a headless doll decorated with a pentagram—often used as a satanic symbol—oddly shaped knives, body paints and wooden crosses which Telb said proved a cult had been active in the half-acre area where deputies dug.

The sheriff said he will continue looking for Charity Freeman, a 7-year-old girl who was reported missing two years ago. Telb said his sources—whom he has never named—told him Charity was killed by a cult headed by her grandfather, Leroy, who has been charged with child stealing.

However, Telb said if the investigation continues, it will be done with "utmost secrecy" to avoid media attention.

The media attention was needed when the dig began, he said then, to scare the cult and prevent another sacrifice on June 21 or 22, when he said satanists mark the summer solstice.

Some township residents believe the search should go on.

"Since I've been out here, there have been some activities that's not quite kosher," said Eli Bias, who has lived in the township since 1956.

"It has always been talked of. They always just say people were seeing ghosts out here. Well, some people don't believe in ghosts, and they was seeing something," Bias said.

"What they should do is restart the investigation, because if it was your kid being snatched, you'd feel differently about it."

Others, including township trustees who believe their community has been slandered by tales of satan-worshippers, scoff at any suggestion of the occult.

"I think this is a bunch of baloney, it is," said Rosella Pepper, who wants to buy the dilapidated house next to one dig site.

The owner of the house has protested that television coverage of the dig will lower his property values, but Ms. Pepper believes there is no reason not to move to the alleged sacrificial site.

"Hell no, I'd move right in. There ain't nothing out there," Pepper said. "I think it's stupid. It's just a big joke."

When authorities came up empty-handed, they tried distancing themselves from the claim that a satanic cult was active in the area. *From* The Cincinnati Enquirer, *Tuesday, July 16, 1985.*

he believed the information to be factual. Telb refused to provide any of that information and continued digging the entire day, unearthing odd things like red string, a doll nailed to a piece of wood and body paint—but no bodies. The following morning, Wednesday, July 3, a spokesman for Sheriff Telb quietly told reporters, "The Lucas County Sheriff's Department has ended its search for victims of a cult." They went on to say that while the department "will keep investigating the disappearance of a seven-year-old girl whose grandfather has been linked to the cult," they were no longer

The devil, you say

Begone, sheriff! Dig for bodies infuriates trustee

Lucas County Sheriff James Telb's search for the devil angered area residents. *From* The Plain Dealer, *Sunday, July 7, 1985.*

looking for any evidence of cult activity. Despite a multiday dig across multiple sites that had been identified as graves, no human remains were recovered.

In July 1985, Alvin and Patricia Litton sued Lucas County Sheriff James Telb for $1.5 million, alleging that they and their five children suffered severe emotional distress, false imprisonment, invasion of privacy, defamation and trespass, all as a result of the raid on their house and subsequent statements made during press conferences. The ink was barely dry on that lawsuit when Edward and Laretta Never filed their own suit against Telb, seeking $975,000 in damages for defamation because Telb had publicly referred to the Never residence as a "cult house" during a press conference. Both lawsuits were filed with the Lucas County Common Pleas Court, but their outcomes are not known, leading many to believe they were dismissed.

On Friday, October 21, 1988, police acting on a tip from the FBI knocked on the door of a Huntington Beach, California apartment. After a few moments, the door was opened by thirteen-year-old Charity Freeman, and the six-year search was over. Charity's grandfather Leroy Freeman was arrested under suspicion of kidnapping and unlawful flight to avoid prosecution. Charity told authorities that back in September 1982, her mother, Karen Croswell, and Freeman had been arguing over how Charity was being raised. It was at that time that Freeman abducted her.

Freeman was extradited to Ohio, and on December 14, 1988, he pled guilty to the charge of child stealing. He was sentenced to four to fifteen years in prison. No evidence was ever found that Leroy Freeman was the leader of a satanic cult or involved in any cult activity.

PART IV

LEGENDARY PLACES

CHAPTER 1

DEEP DIVE INTO THE BLUE HOLE

Long before I moved to Ohio in 1999, I was afraid of the Blue Hole. Mind you, that was the Blue Hole in the Pine Barrens of New Jersey. My dad used to try to scare me with stories of a bottomless pit of bright blue water, haunted by the countless victims who were foolish enough to venture too close to the water's edge or even willingly take up a dare and try to swim in the icy waters. That's because, according to my dad, those people would get pulled down to their watery graves, many never to be seen again. As for who or what was responsible for the snatching, my dad was incredibly vague, although I know for a fact that he tried to blame the Jersey Devil more than a few times. No matter who was to blame, I was always terrified that I would somehow find myself in the Pine Barrens, only to stumble too close to the Blue Hole. So when I moved to Ohio, while I was initially terrified to find there was a Blue Hole here, I relaxed when I learned it wasn't supposed to be haunted. In fact, for many years, it was a roadside tourist trap.

Located in Castalia, Ohio, the Blue Hole is said to have formed inside an abandoned limestone quarry. Beginning in the nineteenth century, the area was a mecca for limestone mining. When mining ceased in the early twentieth century, the quarries were abandoned. In the case of the Blue Hole, groundwater began to fill up the empty quarry, resulting in the pond that rose to fame. What made this pond different from all the other ordinary quarry ponds was its bright blue color, due to the high mineral content and purity of the groundwater.

For as long as any locals could remember, the Blue Hole had been the place to go for a swim or a nice picnic along the water's edge. And really, that's all it needed to be. However, around the 1920s, property owners noticed increased traffic out front. People were driving right past on the way to or returning from Sandusky, Lake Erie and that little amusement park, Cedar Point. If only there were some way to make them all stop for a bit, maybe even spend a few dollars. Sure, the appeal of seeing the picturesque view of the bright blue pond was all well and good, but what was needed was a mysterious backstory. Maybe the water was bottomless, or there were hidden caverns dotting the property? Now you're talking! Put in a public restroom and a gift shop, and you have a bona fide tourist trap!

And that's precisely what happened. In the 1920s, the Blue Hole was an official pit stop where people could get out, stretch their legs and look at some blue water. The stories about the water being bottomless and every attempt to find the bottom proving fruitless were just that: stories. The kernel of truth was that they never could determine the exact measure of the water's depth, but that had more to do with the fluctuating groundwater that fed the hole, causing the water level to rise and fall, than anything else. It's generally

An assortment of Blue Hole memorabilia from the author's collection. *Author photo.*

accepted that the water was between forty-two and forty-five feet deep. But that takes some of the mystery out of it, so when the Blue Hole gift shop started selling postcards, the backs of all of them noted that the actual depth of the Blue Hole "is unknown."

Over the years, as more and more people stopped by to marvel at the Blue Hole, the decision was made that it probably wasn't a good idea to let people continue to swim in it, so a wooden fence was erected around the entire pond, where people could stop and gaze out at the waters. Of course, there were always a few adventuresome individuals who would still try to sneak and dip a toe in when they thought no one was looking. It seemed that there were new arrivals to the gift shop almost weekly, with photos and illustrations of the Blue Hole emblazoned across everything from shirts and hats to salt and pepper shakers and ashtrays. At the height of its popularity, well over 150,000 people a year were stopping by the Blue Hole. It was featured in numerous newspapers, local and national, as well as in travel brochures.

As time wore on and the back roads were forsaken for the speed of interstate travel, tourist traps everywhere began to see their visitor numbers dwindle. The Blue Hole was no exception. It hung on as long as possible, but the Blue Hole closed in the 1990s. The property was purchased by the Castalia Trout Club and is no longer open to the public. The archway that cars drove through to get to the Blue Hole is still visible, although the gate itself is locked and a "Keep Out" sign is posted.

CHAPTER 2

THE LOOKOUT ON JOHNSON'S ISLAND

It's easy to dismiss the Buckeye State's role in the Civil War simply because only a few minor battles took place in Ohio. Often overlooked is the fact that Ohio supplied over three hundred thousand soldiers. What's more, since Ohio was centrally located within the Union states, it served as a central hub for the transportation of everything from supplies to Confederate prisoners of war, many of whom ended up being held in Ohio prisoner of war camps. Nestled quietly in Sandusky Bay, along the shores of Lake Erie, there's an island that was once home to over ten thousand Confederate prisoners of war: Johnson's Island.

The earliest records of the three-hundred-acre island, dating to 1809, refer to it as Bull's Island, after its original owner, Epaphras W. Bull, in 1809. It acquired its current name around 1852, when Bull sold the property to L.B. Johnson. Until then, the island was privately owned and used for primary or secondary residences, so there were not many houses and lots of woods. The Civil War would change all that.

In 1861, shortly after the War Between the States broke out, Johnson's Island was brought to the attention of U.S. officials, who were seeking a location for a new prison camp. While Ohio already had several Confederate prisoner of war camps, most notably Camp Chase in Columbus, the federal government was looking for a suitable location to construct a prison camp specifically designed to hold captured Confederate officers. When officials visited Johnson's Island, they knew they had found what they were looking for. The island was far enough out in Sandusky Bay to make escapes futile yet close enough to Sandusky that supply lines could still be maintained.

Entrance to Johnson's Island Confederate Stockade Cemetery. *Author photo.*

In 1862, the United States government leased a portion of Johnson's Island for $500 a year. Construction on the prison stockade began almost immediately, using wood cut from the trees on the island itself. Work progressed quickly, and before long, the facility was completed. The centerpiece was the prison area. It was designed to be self-sufficient and included twelve two-story prisoner barracks, two mess halls, a hospital, a recreation area and three wells, all surrounded by a fifteen-foot-high wooden stockade. Outside the stockade walls were close to forty buildings for the 128th Ohio Infantry Regiment, which would be tasked with guarding the prison camp. The 128th had its own barracks, stables, latrines—even a store. And while it was hoped that it wouldn't need to be used, a small area was set aside for a cemetery. Altogether, the prison site took up almost seventeen of the three hundred total acres on Johnson's Island.

In April 1862, the prison officially opened, and the first prisoners to arrive were Confederate officers shipped up from Camp Chase in Columbus. While Johnson's Island was the only prisoner of war camp designed to hold exclusively Confederate officers, it would eventually take in privates, spies and even civilians. Roughly a month after the prison opened, on May 25, 1862, Confederate Lieutenant R.M. Ray became the first recorded person to die on Johnson's island. He would not be the last.

The archway one must pass under to enter Johnson's Island Confederate Stockade Cemetery. *Author photo.*

The reason for this became apparent as the summer of 1862 turned to fall. That's around when the Southern Confederate soldiers got their first taste of Northern Ohio cold weather. On top of that, the winds blowing across Lake Erie often caused the temperature to quickly drop below freezing. By and large, Confederate soldiers were not used to the Northern climate. They tried to huddle under blankets and did anything possible to keep warm, but as soon as winter came, the winds started to pick up and the snow began to fall, prisoners began to die. To make matters worse, the freezing temperatures and snow so frequently recorded in and around Johnson's Island often made supply runs impossible, so food and medical supplies became scarce. Sadly, as more and more Confederate soldiers passed away, the cemetery, which had initially been only a small plot of land, began to grow in size to accommodate all the bodies.

Johnson's Island would remain in operation through the end of the Civil War, officially closing in September 1865. In the four years that it was in operation, an estimated 10,000 to 15,000 Confederate officers were housed, at one time or another, on Johnson's Island. As for the Confederate cemetery, officially, there are 206 people buried there, though some put the number closer to 300. The reasons for this are poor recordkeeping and the original grave markers, which were made of wood, deteriorating. On top of that, there are several markers labelled simply "Unknown," as well as various stones and broken pieces of wood with no markings on them, leaving it a mystery whether they are grave markers or not.

After the soldiers were released at the war's end, the Johnson's Island stockade was closed, and the buildings were abandoned. The federal government would eventually sell the island off and put it under private ownership. Interestingly enough, in the 1890s, there was an attempt to turn the property where the stockade stood into a resort that could compete with the newly opened Cedar Point. The facility, named the Johnson's Island Pleasure Resort, used portions of the abandoned stockade to help create some of the resort's outbuildings. However, the resort's owners quickly found they couldn't compete with Cedar Point, and in 1908, the entire Johnson's Island Pleasure Resort was sold to Cedar Point for what amounted to $800 in stock.

Once the sale was complete, Cedar Point moved or razed all the buildings. As for the Johnson's Island cemetery, that was purchased by the United Daughters of the Confederacy of Cincinnati the same year Cedar Point purchased the resort. It was the United Daughters of the Confederacy of Cincinnati who began restoration work by replacing as many missing and

Above: Graves of Confederate soldiers buried at Johnson's Island Confederate Stockade Cemetery. *Author photo.*

Left: *The Lookout*, sculpted by Moses Ezekiel, stands watch over the cemetery. *Author photo.*

broken grave markers as possible and attempting to identify any unmarked graves. They also placed a more permanent fence around the boundaries of the cemetery. In 1910, American sculptor Moses Ezekiel unveiled *The Lookout*, a bronze sculpture of a Confederate soldier standing on a granite base in the center of the cemetery. In his right hand, the soldier holds a gun with a bayonet, the butt of which rests by his feet. His left hand is raised to his hat, shading his eyes as he scans the horizon.

In 1975, Johnson's Island was officially designated a National Historic Landmark, and plans were set in motion to continue preserving as much of the island's history as possible. Today, while numerous private residences dot Johnson's Island, the cemetery is still easily accessible and open to the public. Other historical markers and descriptors have been added where the prison once stood, and the island hosts educational tours and reenactments, all to continue raising awareness of the impact a small island in Sandusky Bay had during the U.S. Civil War.

CHAPTER 3

ROGUES HOLLOW

Believe it or not, there is a place in Ohio called Rogues Hollow—and yes, it's supposed to be haunted by a whole host of spirits, including, as far as I can tell, Ohio's only headless horse. It is said that during its heyday, Rogues Hollow was a place few people dared to tread, especially after dark, and not only because of the ghosts. That's because the people who called Rogues Hollow their home were said to live up to the town's name. But just how much of this story is true? Let's walk down into the Hollow to find out—if you dare!

The remains of Rogues Hollow lie about a mile or so south of the village of Doylestown in Wayne County. Doylestown was founded in 1827 by a man who settled there, William Doyle. He loved the rolling hills of the area and the streams that crisscrossed it, too. It was perfect for sheep farmers, who started populating the area and later added mills along the streams. It was an idyllic life, and when people weren't naming villages after themselves, they were assigning descriptive names to them, such as Peacock Hollow, since the view was as pretty as a peacock.

In the early 1840s, coal was discovered in and around the hollows of Doylestown. And while, at least initially, the village of Doylestown remained the same, over time there was a large influx of coal miners looking for work. Even today, coal mining is not a job for the faint of heart. Things were even worse back in the 1840s. Men working the coal mines had to deal with the ever-present danger of mine collapses and accidents, which could mean the loss of a limb or a life. Suffice it to say, coal miners worked hard, and they played hard, too. Initially, Doylestown had only one tavern, which was soon overrun with workers from the neighboring coal mines. Doylestown tried to keep up by opening several more taverns, but even that wasn't enough to deal with the influx of thirsty patrons. Then one day, the tavernkeepers in Doylestown noticed that the crowds had started to dwindle a bit, especially in the evenings, when their establishments were usually the most crowded. Turns out the miners were all heading out to Peacock Hollow, where two new taverns had just opened up. Truthfully, there wasn't much out in Peacock Hollow besides a mill and something resembling a general store. But then a third tavern opened up and then a fourth. Eventually, there would be seven taverns erected in the hollow. And that's when people started referring to the location as Rogues Hollow.

Now, some historians will state that the name came from a man who settled there by the last name of Rogue. Further confusing matters is the different ways people punctuate the hollow's name; sometimes it's "Rogue's," other times "Rogues'" and sometimes there's no apostrophe at all and it's just "Rogues." But most will say the hollow's name describes the type of characters you would likely encounter there: rogues—dishonest, destructive and often violent.

While the names of the first few taverns were relatively tame (they were no doubt named after their owners: Walsh's Saloon, for example), the names grew more colorful with each new tavern that opened up. Along with that came more interesting ways to pass the time inside the tavern. If a simple card game was a bit too tame for your liking, there was gambling of all sorts that could be found if you knew where to look. There was also cockfighting and even dogfighting, if that was more your speed. And if you were looking to get into a fight, it was said all you needed to do was walk in the door of Billy Gallagher's aptly named Devil's Den. In its heyday, the word around Rogues Hollow was that everybody who went into Devil's Den looking for a fight found one, but only half of them ever came back out afterward.

Well, if they never came back out, where did they go? There was a running joke surrounding Rogues Hollow: "People don't die in Rogues Hollow; they just disappear from Rogues Hollow." True or not, rumors like this fueled the idea that many of these missing people were found dead at the bottom of one of the coal mines. Indeed, it wasn't too far of a stretch to imagine someone who had had a few drinks too many attempting to stumble home and accidentally falling into a mine shaft. That was the mindset of anyone who set foot in Rogues Hollow: if someone was found at the bottom of a mine shaft, they died from accidentally falling in. Rare was the time when anyone decided to try to determine if someone was dead before they hit the bottom. The mines were occasionally used to hide more than bodies. Long after the coal mines closed down and the buildings of Rogues Hollow were all but abandoned, stolen merchandise was still being pulled from the mines.

Russell Frey chronicled the history and legends of Rogues Hollow in this book, from the author's collection. *Author photo.*

Most of what we know about the ghosts of Rogues' Hollow comes from a book by Russell W. Frey, self-published in 1958: *Rogues' Hollow: History and Legends*. For this book, Frey collected old news articles and spoke to several, as he referred to them, "old-timers," who shared the stories as they had been told to them. It should be noted that Frey's book contains only a few first-person stories, meaning the bulk of the tales he included might have changed substantially prior to his committing them to paper—which brings us to the ghost stories.

Given the number of unsavory things that happened in the many taverns of Rogues Hollow, it stands to reason that those buildings would be the most haunted places there. Unfortunately, little remains of the taverns, so we turn to the mines themselves, where men worked and sometimes died. Even at night, people walking past the mines have reported hearing the sounds of miners working. Russell Frey's book even includes accounts of people seeing ghostly miners emerging from the mine and disappearing into the distance, almost as if they are returning home after a long day of work.

One of the well-known ghost stories associated with Rogues Hollow is that of the ghost of a young boy who is said to haunt Sam Chidester's mill. Legend has it that the boy was working at the mill when he was accidentally crushed to death. The night after the boy's death, a group of men walking past Chidester's Mill saw what looked to be the ghostly face of a young boy peeking out a window at them. Not ones to be easily spooked, the men were ready to write off the incident as nothing more than a trick of the moonlight on a windowpane—that is, until they heard others describe seeing the same ghost looking out the mill's windows. The sightings continue today, perhaps because Chidester's Mill is one of the few original Rogues Hollow buildings still standing.

Far and away the creepiest ghost story connected to Rogues Hollow involves a spooky old tree, which Frey calls the Ghost Oak Tree. Sightings in and around this tree are widespread and include ghosts, strange creatures and even the Devil, who likes to hide in the tree and jump down onto unsuspecting victims. Stranger still, the Devil will sometimes suddenly appear, sitting on a headless horse. Not content to stand there, the headless horse, with its devilish rider in tow, roams through the area where Rogues Hollow's taverns once stood. Other times, the horse stands next to the tree with nary a devil in sight.

Today, very little remains of Rogues Hollow. The area is owned and maintained by the Chippewa-Rogues' Hollow Historical Society, which is housed inside Chidester's Mill. While it is closed in the winter, it is open for tours during the spring and summer. So make your plans to visit now. But if you should find yourself face-to-face with the Devil and a headless horse, don't say I didn't warn you!

CHAPTER 4

BURIED TREASURE ON THE GREAT TRAIL

When one's deciding where to search for buried treasure, Ohio probably isn't a location that springs to the top of the list. Pity, because historical documentation suggests that an enormous pile of gold and silver—so much that it took sixteen horses to carry it all—was buried somewhere along the Great Trail near Minerva. Is it still there? Well, grab a shovel, and let's see what we can find.

Before the treasure was buried, it resided in the French-occupied Fort Duquesne, in Pittsburgh, Pennsylvania. It was earmarked for the French soldiers fighting in the French and Indian War, which was well underway. It is said that British troops were pushing toward Fort Duquesne, greatly outnumbering those defending the fort. Rather than let all the gold and silver fall into the hands of the enemy, a plan was devised to get the treasure out of Fort Duquesne and back into the hands of the French.

The plan was for a small group of soldiers to sneak out of the fort under cover of darkness with as much of the gold and silver as they could carry. The hope was that they could follow the Tuscawaras Trail, also known as the Great Trail, which would lead them to French-occupied Fort Detroit. If, for some reason, the men couldn't make it to Fort Detroit or were in danger of being taken prisoner, they were instructed to bury the gold and silver as quickly as possible, making sure to leave behind clues so that it could be recovered at a later date.

Late one evening, the gold and silver was loaded onto packhorses, sixteen in all, and ten men led the way out of Fort Duquesne and onto the Great

Trail, heading west. The journey started out well enough, and the days passed without incident as the group continued west, eventually crossing into Ohio, where they started following the trail in a northwesterly fashion. But then a scout, who had been sent ahead to check for enemy troops, reported back that a column of British soldiers was approaching from the north.

On hearing the news, the French commander ordered his men to bury the treasure immediately, as per their orders before leaving Fort Duquesne. They needed to work quickly, but they also knew they had to pick a special place to bury the treasure so they could leave clues about its whereabouts that were easy to follow. They chose to dig a hole "in the center of a square bounded by four small springs." The ten men had barely enough time to bury all the gold and silver before the British were almost upon them. So the men decided to run and hide until the British had passed through the area. Then they would return and leave clues about where the treasure was hidden.

Unfortunately, the men were quickly cornered by the British, who killed or took prisoner all but two of the French soldiers, who had managed to remain hidden. Once the coast was clear, the two men quickly set about creating clues that would aid in recovering the treasure. Some thought was given to digging up the treasure and resuming the trip to Fort Detroit, but that idea was quickly abandoned, as there were only two of them and the British had taken all the packhorses with them.

So the two men set about creating clues that would lead to the treasure, and one of the men wrote it all down in a letter. Knowing that the treasure was already bounded by four springs, the men decided to create markers that would help lead them back to its location, should their return be delayed and the terrain change. To the east of the treasure, the men carved the figure of a deer into a tree. To the west, they forced an oddly shaped rock into a fork in a tree. Finally, they hid their shovels under a fallen tree to the north. Once someone found the shovels, they would need to walk six hundred steps to the south, and they would be standing right on top of the gold. And if they took the newly found shovels with them, they'd already have a means to dig up the treasure. When the men had finished their work and committed their clues to the letter, they simply walked away. And just like that, the two men and their clue-filled letter promptly faded into obscurity.

After the French and Indian War ended in 1763, not much was said about the buried treasure or the fact that there were clues to finding it. Like all good buried treasure tales, the story of the treasure of the Great Trail quickly slipped from fact into legend. Depending on who was telling you the story, the treasure never really existed, or it did, but it was recovered a long time ago. Of course, the best version of the story claimed that the treasure was real and still out there, waiting for someone to gain possession of the handwritten letter that contained the clues leading to it.

It seemed the wait might be over when, in 1829, a man walked into Minerva and proudly proclaimed that he had the letter with the clues. The man said he came to possess the letter because his uncle had written it. When asked why the uncle hadn't just gone out there and retrieved the treasure himself, the mysterious stranger said, "It was too dangerous," and left it at that.

Most people didn't think too much about this stranger and the wild story he told. If he had the clues to finding the treasure, he should have dug it up and kept his mouth shut about it. It was even stranger when the man willingly gave up what all the clues were. That doesn't seem to be a good way of recovering missing treasure without going missing yourself at the hands of some unsavory characters who want the treasure all to themselves. True or not, the specific clues that led to the treasure came from this stranger. As to whether or not he ever found anything, no one is sure, because he just stopped showing up in town.

Seeks Buried Gold, Silver Near Minerva

MINERVA, July 28. — (AP) — A modern prospector with a divining rod is all set to start digging for 16 pack horse loads of gold and silver—if he can just find a map.

He's offering a $1000 reward for it.

Charles Widener, of Minerva, isn't worried about 175 years of dirt he may have to shovel before he strikes the million-dollar treasure. He figures he has a lifetime to work.

More than 170 years after the fact, people were still looking for the legendary Minerva Gold. *From* The Dayton Daily News, *Sunday, July 29, 1951.*

While most were content to chalk the whole thing up to being a legend, something strange started happening every few years: someone would inadvertently stumble across one of the clues. A man claimed he was out chopping down a tree when a weird-looking rock that had been wedged into one of the tree's forks fell to the ground. Another time, someone clearing fallen trees from the area unearthed several rusty shovels. And then there was the time someone found a faded carving of a deer in the side of a tree. All that, but still no one said they'd found the treasure.

The last known "official" treasure hunt happened in 1951, when Minerva resident Charles Widener, twenty-nine, offered $1,000 for any map that could help him find the treasure. Widener, who referred to himself as a "modern-day prospector," clearly could have used some help, because he used only a set of dowsing rods while treasure hunting.

What do you think? Does the treasure exist? And if it did, is it long gone, having been dug up ages ago? Or maybe, just maybe, it's still out there. And if it is, what are you waiting for? You've got all the clues. Get out there and find it!

PART V

THE UNEXPLAINED

CHAPTER 1

THE WEREWOLVES OF DEFIANCE

I've never really felt comfortable around werewolf legends, myself. It doesn't matter if you try to disguise it by calling it a dogman. There's just something so violent and visceral about a werewolf that I know I wouldn't have a chance if I ran up against one. They're always wandering, too. Ghosts tend to haunt specific areas. Not werewolves: they're always on the move, which means there could be one working its way toward me right now, and I wouldn't even know it until it was too late. Honestly, I'm a big Warren Zevon fan, and I'm convinced he's singing out a warning that was meant for me and me alone in his song "Werewolves of London": "You better stay away from him / He'll rip your lungs out, Jim." That's why, when I decided to look into the history of the Defiance Werewolf, I told myself it was just a one-off event confined to Defiance. Oh, how wrong I was!

The first documented sighting of what would become known as the Defiance Werewolf happened on the evening of July 25, 1972, at the Norfolk and Western Train Yard in Defiance. Railroad worker Ted Davis was walking alongside the trains when he saw "huge hairy feet" in front of him. Looking up, Davis saw a hairy creature, at least six feet tall, standing before him. Worse, the beast had a big stick or board in its hands. As Davis stared at the creature, trying to process what he was seeing, the beast swung the stick at Davis, hitting him in the shoulder. The creature then ran off, and as it did, Davis noted it appeared to be wearing blue jeans.

The next sighting took place several days later, again at the Defiance train yard, and Ted Davis was involved once again. This time, though, he wasn't alone. Davis was talking with his coworker Tom Jones when he saw the creature at the far end of the yard, near the main tracks. Jones later confirmed it was the same creature Davis had seen a few nights earlier, right down to the blue jeans. They could both also see that the creature appeared to have fangs. As they continued to watch the beast, it seemed to grow agitated and started running from side to side. That was all Davis and Jones needed to see, and they ran back to the depot. Unsure of what to do, the two men called the local police department and filed a report. Several days later, the *Toledo Blade* got ahold of the story and published an article about the attacks in the August 2 edition of the paper. And with that, werewolf fever struck Defiance, Ohio.

The article featured comments from Defiance Police Chief Donald Breckler, who attempted to downplay the events while assuring residents that the police department was taking them seriously, and one quote really caused a stir: "We're concerned for the safety of our people." That was all the good people of Defiance needed to hear, and suddenly, there were sightings of the werewolf everywhere. It was rattling doorknobs and scratching at doors on the north side of Defiance one night and jumping out in front of cars driven by grocery store employees the next. Defiance police officials kept telling residents that while they were taking the reports seriously, there was no cause for alarm, as they had yet to confirm that an actual werewolf was running around the area. They also began to subtly hint that perhaps a few of the sightings were hoaxes or practical jokes, something they had to strongly discourage, especially when some residents started carrying loaded firearms around with them for protection.

The werewolf sightings in Defiance had died down considerably by the first week of August 1972. Some say the initial sightings were just practical jokes that got out of hand, and when the whole town started believing in the werewolf, the prankster just stopped. Others thought the creature was an actual person, someone riding the rails, which would explain why he was carrying a weapon and why the sightings stopped as suddenly as they began. However, some say the sightings stopped in Defiance because the werewolf migrated out of the area.

Looking back at newspaper articles from the time, it seems that even some reporters thought the Defiance werewolf was migrating, as evidenced by the first line in an article from the August 4 edition of the Findlay *Republican-Courier*: "The Defiance werewolf may have hopped a freight train for Tiffin." The article says that on the evening of August 3, a man saw a "hunched ape-like animal" walking around in the woods near Tiffin, Ohio. The man

Bela Lugosi Go Home

Citizens Jumpy Over 'Werewolf'

DEFIANCE — In the aftermath of the sighting of a wolf-like creature several days ago in Defiance, dozens of other reported sightings are pouring into the offices of the Defiance Police Department and the Defiance County Sheriff's Department.

Several persons have reported being attacked by a wolf-like creature.

"This whole thing is amazing," said a police dispatcher who handles calls for both departments. "People are jumping when they hear noises." After they jump, they apparently also reach for the nearest telephone and call the closest law enforcement agency. "It's getting out of hand," the weary dispatcher said

A man reported Thursday night that he experienced "a feeling it was following him" while a woman reported it rattled her front door.

Police had dubbed the object of their investigations the "wolf man" because they believe the person to be wearing a mask. They theorized the motive of the incidents could have been robbery or just to scare people.

Despite a similar report from Seneca County, miles to the east of Defiance, surrounding counties have seen no werewolf or wolf man.

After the initial werewolf sighting, reports continued to come in from across Defiance. *From* The Van Wert Times Bulletin, *Saturday, August 5, 1972.*

described to the Seneca County Sheriff's Office that the animal was "very hairy, six or seven feet tall, with wolf-like ears and fangs." The man told police he took one look at the creature and ran. Can't say I blame him.

Rumors spread around Carey, Ohio, that a small boy had encountered a wolflike creature while playing in Carey Memorial Park. The rumor created a bit of a panic in Carey, so much so that Police Chief Vincent Jacob issued a statement saying his department had not received a single report of any werewolf or wolflike creature anywhere in or around Carey. "I think the whole thing is a hoax, myself," Jacob said.

On Wednesday, August 9, "that big, hairy and ugly creature that some people think has been roaming Northwestern Ohio" was seen in northern Wyandot County. A woman reported to the sheriff's office that while she was out driving, "a big, black thing jumped out of a ditch right beside her car." This report didn't call the creature a werewolf but rather a "hair monster," and its description doesn't seem to fit that of the other werewolf sightings. Still, the article did try to tie them together, but perhaps that's just for the sake of simplicity.

The Monday, August 28 edition of the *Telegraph-Forum* said that over the weekend, residents of Plymouth, Ohio, reported seeing a werewolf-like creature described as "weighing about 275 pounds, wearing shoes, hairy and six feet tall." As this creature ran around Plymouth, it was seen tearing a screen off a house, scaring "three 15-year-old boys to death" and even jumping over a fence in a single bound.

Like the Defiance sightings, the Northern Ohio sightings of 1972 had fizzled out by the start of winter. Looking back at all the reports, one is left with many questions, not the least of which is: Where did this creature come from? And where did it go? Well, if it did exist, here's one possible answer to both questions. In the late 1800s, in the town of Delphos, Ohio, roughly thirty miles south of Defiance, there were reports of wolflike creatures roaming around near Resurrection Cemetery. Even the local priest reported seeing them. The cemetery and the swampy area around it were said to be the "home" of these creatures. While most thought the sightings were of actual wolves, could it be that Delphos, Ohio, really is home base for werewolves? And that maybe the one that terrorized Defiance and the surrounding area in 1972 originated from Delphos and was just out riding the rails for a bit of a vacation? Anything's possible. As for me, I'm not taking any chances and am steering clear of Delphos's Resurrection Cemetery. You know, because of the whole "ripping your lungs out" bit.

CHAPTER 2
THE MELONHEADS OF WISNER ROAD

One of the things I love about Ohioans is that they are never satisfied with having "normal" stuff like all the other states. Nowhere is this more apparent than in their urban legends and creatures. Sure, Ohio has Bigfoot, Hook Man and Crybaby Bridges, but the Buckeye State needs unique creatures it can call its own. Case in point: the Melonheads.

While there have been whispers of the Melonheads throughout Northern Ohio since the 1960s, pinning down the original story is almost impossible. There are stories of Melonheads originating from numerous places across Northern Ohio, including Mentor, Kirtland and Chardon. By and large, the location most often mentioned as the home of the Melonheads legend is Wisner Road, which winds its way through Chardon Township. Driving on Wisner Road, you can immediately see why the stories ended up settling in here; it's a worn-down road with rows of spooky trees on either side, forming a canopy. You'll know you are getting close when you must cross the Crybaby Bridge to reach the dead end. That's when the fun begins!

There are two versions of the Melonheads legend, both involving the mysterious Dr. Crowe. In the nicer, and therefore not as popular, legend, Dr. Crowe had a house or small orphanage in the woods at the end of the road. Crowe worked for the government, as the story goes, and he was asked to care for a small group of orphans who were all stricken with hydrocephalus: "water on the brain." This disease caused the children's heads to swell, which is how they became known as the Melonheads. It is said that one night, the doctor passed away in his sleep. Unsure of what

Left: Stop! Melonheads ahead! *Author photo.*

Below: When you see this sign, you'll know you're entering Melonhead Country. *Author photo.*

Opposite: The woods where the Melonheads are said to lurk, waiting. *Author photo.*

to do, the Melonheads decided to bury the good doctor on the property and remain where they were. When they failed to keep up with repairs on their house, it fell into disrepair, eventually collapsing and leaving nothing save the stone foundation. If you've heard this version of the story, you know that if you want to see the Melonheads for yourself, you must drive down to the end of Wisner Road, park your car and wait. Eventually, the Melonheads will come creeping out of the woods and stand by the side of the road, just staring at you.

It's a weird story, but it's not very scary. That's why this next version is the most popular one. Here, while we still have Dr. Crowe, he's not nice. While he also worked for the government in this version, his job was to perform "hellish experiments" on orphans he kept chained and locked in cages in the basement of his house, again located at the end of Wisner Road. Because of these experiments, the orphans' heads became misshapen, and their teeth became sharp and fang-like. One night, the Melonheads were able to escape their chains and attacked the doctor, killing him, and burned down the house. Once they were done, the Melonheads disappeared into the woods surrounding Wisner Road. This version is the more popular one because teenagers and thrill-seekers of all ages like parking their car at the end of Wisner Road late at night and daring one another to get out of the car and stand at the edge of the woods. That's what you need to do to see the Melonheads, who will come rushing out of the woods and try

When you see the Crybaby Bridge, you're getting close. *Author photo.*

to attack you. Even if you return to the safety of the car, you're not in the clear yet, as the Melonheads will jump on your car and try to scratch and claw their way in.

It's a creepy story, to be sure. The problem is, I have yet to find a single piece of historical documentation showing that there ever was a Dr. Crowe, at least one who had a residence at the end of Wisner Road. The closest I've come to date was that I did find a Dr. Crowe near Mentor-on-the-Lake, and I even managed to find what locals say is his tombstone. It's not; it's just a house marker that sits near the curb. There's also the possibility that a Dr. Crowe might have spent some time in a small cabin off Wisner Road—but no experiments and certainly no Melonheads. That hasn't stopped the reports of people claiming to have encountered Melonheads on Wisner Road. Primarily, they are described as small, almost childlike individuals with deformed heads. Sometimes, the Melonheads have glowing eyes, and they've been known to let out high-pitched screams to communicate with each other. I have heard first-person accounts of such encounters dozens of times over the years, enough times that I must admit that, at the very least, these individuals think they've witnessed a Melonhead. I myself have been up and down Wisner Road many times and have yet to see anything out of the ordinary, leading me to surmise that perhaps the Melonheads have

The Wisner Road Crybaby Bridge, in all its glory. *Author photo.*

picked up and moved. Where? Well, Melonhead stories are now coming out of Holland, Michigan. The Michigan stories are incredibly similar, right down to legend trippers needing to go down a path through the woods to reach the home/lair of Dr. Crowe. Of course, things get a little suspicious when you realize that Dr. Crowe's "abandoned" former home is the Felt Mansion, which is available for wedding bookings.

CHAPTER 3

THE THING FROM CHARLES MILL LAKE

On the evening of Thursday, March 26, 1959, three Mansfield teenagers, Wayne Armstrong (sixteen), Michael Lane (fourteen) and Denny Patterson (sixteen), were driving around in Armstrong's car, looking for something to do. The fog started rolling in as the teens drove around, and the temperature began to drop, just as in any good monster movie. That's when the three noticed they were close to Charles Mill Lake, a sprawling reservoir with nearly 1,350 acres of water and twenty-five miles of shoreline stretching across two counties, Ashland and Richland. The teens figured the fog would probably be thick and spooky-looking rolling in off the lake water, so they headed in that direction.

When they got to the main road into the lake area, they started looking for a way to drive close to the water's edge. Eventually, they found what they would later describe as a lane that took them down to a boathouse. They found they could drive down almost to the water's edge as they passed beside the boathouse. Parking at the end of the lane, facing the water, they sat quietly and watched the fog roll in. As they watched, one of the boys pointed out a large log lying near the water. But then the "log" stood up, and chaos ensued as the panic-stricken boys tried to get out of there posthaste. Michael Lane would later describe to the *News Journal* how "the Thing stood up and was about seven feet tall, had no arms and two green eyes. Then it started walking towards the car." Wayne Armstrong, who was still behind the wheel, didn't see how close the creature got to his car, as he was too busy trying to get the vehicle turned around so they could escape. Lane saw it, though, and would later say it got pretty close, "about 15 feet away," before Armstrong could get the car facing away from the lake—and the armless creature with green eyes—and the teens escaped unscathed.

Hightailing it back to Mansfield, Armstrong, Lane and Peterson came across a mutual friend, Dave Owens. The trio told Owens about the strange creature they had just seen, but he was, understandably, skeptical. To convince Owens that the monster was real, they all piled back into Armstrong's car and headed back out to Charles Mill Lake. Unfortunately, when they returned to the spot, the creature was gone. So was the "log" they had initially seen, which they all found a bit curious. Feeling somewhat relieved and maybe a bit rejected, the teenage monster hunters went home and went to bed.

The following morning, when the teens told Wayne's father, Harold Armstrong, what they'd encountered at Charles Mill Lake, he just laughed and told them there was no such thing as monsters. The boys persisted, and Harold Armstrong finally told them, "Prove it." If there really was a seven-foot-tall monster lumbering around the shoreline of Charles Mill Lake, surely it would have left behind footprints. Why not go out there and look for some? With that, the three teens and Harold Armstrong drove out to the lake, searching for evidence.

On arriving at Charles Mill Lake, they drove around until they found the lane they had taken down to the boathouse. They parked the car in the same spot as the night before, got out and headed in the direction the creature had come from. Wouldn't you know it: there were at least two big tracks, right where the creature had been standing. Harold Armstrong still wasn't convinced and thought he'd give the teens one more test to see if they were pulling his leg. If the boys thought they had seen a monster and these were its footprints, they should go to the police station and report it. Armstrong was a bit shocked when the teens readily agreed. Off to the police station they went.

The group went back into Mansfield to the police station and made a report. Deputy Thomas Moore of the Richland County Sheriff's Department was at the station and agreed to accompany everyone back to where the alleged monster sighting occurred. When they arrived, Deputy Moore realized that the small road the boys had been parked on was technically in neighboring Ashland County, so he called in the report to that police station. Shortly thereafter, Deputy Charles Myers of the Ashland County Sheriff's Department arrived on the scene. Deputy Meyers thought the monster's footprints resembled the sort of fins or flippers that skin divers

Boys Report Seeing Green-Eyed Monster

Charles Mill Lake may have a counterpart of Scotland's famed Loch Ness Monster.

The story of an all-black monster, six to seven feet tall, with two green eyes and no arms, has been investigated by both Richland and Ashland County Sheriff's deputies after three Mansfield youths said they saw it Thursday night on a lane which leads out to a peninsula in the lake from old State Route 30.

The boys, Michael Lane, 14, of 645 West Longview Ave.; Wayne Armstrong, 16, 656 West Longview Ave., and Denny Patterson, 16, of Lawnsdale Ave., were driving around in the Armstrong youth's car Thursday night. The heavy fog which covered the area gave them the idea of driving down to Charles Mill Lake to see how thick it was over the water, Lane said.

WATCHING FOG

They drove down a lane beside the boathouse and parked their car and were just sitting there watching the thick layers of mist rising from the lake when one of the boys pointed to what they thought was a log lying beside the water.

Suddenly the "log" was getting up from the ground.

"Our hair was standing on end," Lane said. "The 'Thing' stood up and was about seven feet tall, had no arms and two green eyes. Then it started walking toward the car."

"We decided to get out of there fast, but we had trouble getting the car turned around and when we finally did and looked back it was only about 15 feet away."

"We hurried back to Mansfield and found a friend of ours, Dave Owens, and told him about it, but he didn't believe us so he got into the car and we went back to the lake where we had seen it.

(Continued On Page 5)

★

Circus Comes Out Ahead In Race To Space

NEW YORK (AP) — The circus has won the "space" race.

Ringling Bros. Barnum & Bailey shot a midget to the moon Friday night from a launching pad in Madison Square Garden — scoring a beat on all the world's anxious scientists.

The clown act, developed by Paul Jung, was part of the fun and razzle-dazzle circus clientele have come to expect. The 13,500 in the large arena were not disappointed.

★

This is a circus which put the accent not on tinsel, but on the timing of tight-rope walkers. The gaudy glitter of some circuses of the past is held to a minimum, although a lavish procession of "beauties of all ages" is given featured play.

Jugglers perform suspended by their teeth or hair, the unlikeliest of Miss Americas parades in a shocking pink bathing suit and 15 clowns of all sizes and shapes pile from Lou Jacobs' auto, the last clown beating a large yellow drum.

(Continued On Page 5)

The article that introduced Ohio to the Charles Mill Lake Monster. *From* The News Journal, *Saturday, March 28, 1959.*

use and wondered whether perhaps that teens had fallen victim to a hoax or maybe simply misidentified someone out for a late-night dive in Charles Mill Lake. The boys disagreed, claiming that what they saw was not a person: the green eyes were not human.

But they weren't ready to claim it was a monster. Michael Lane thought perhaps they had seen a large bear, as he had heard stories of bear sightings around the area recently. Interestingly, while a bear's eyeshine is usually yellow or orange, it can sometimes appear green.

Whatever the teens encountered that foggy night in 1959, be it man or beast, it rarely, if ever, chose to make a return appearance. While there have been random alleged sightings over the years, no other documented ones exist. In 1985, researcher and cryptozoologist Loren Coleman published a book, *Curious Encounters*, in which he wrote about the Charles Mill Lake Monster, adding, "The thing was seen again in 1963 and described as 'luminous and green-eyed.'" No other specifics are given regarding the 1963 sighting, raising the question of whether it was the same creature. Either way, two sightings over sixty-five years could mean the beast has passed or moved on. Or perhaps it's still out there, waiting for a carload of curious teenagers to come down to the edge of Charles Mill Lake some dark and foggy night.

CHAPTER 3

OL' ORANGE EYES

Having been investigating all things strange and spooky in Ohio since 1999, I've concluded that one of the things that fascinates me the most is also what frustrates me the most. By that I mean the way Ohio truly embraces its weirdness. Having moved to Ohio armed with the most glowing review I could find, "I think a lot of people drive through Ohio," I am proud to say that not only is Ohio weird, but Ohioans also love to share their weirdness. So I can't go very far without someone sharing with me their ghostly tales or the story of the time they saw strange lights in the sky or a large, hairy creature came barreling through the woods toward them.

The frustrating part is that Ohioans, like most people, want everything to make sense and fit together nicely. This is most apparent in the area of cryptids and monsters, where sightings of different creatures get smashed into a sort of amalgam. This frustrates researchers like myself because descriptions and narratives often get rewritten or changed, often for no purpose other than to make all the pieces fit. Everyone loves a good mystery—as long as it comes with a nice, tidy solution with no loose ends. And when the pieces don't fit? Well, just grab yourself a hammer and start whacking that square peg until it fits in the round hole. This happens a lot in Ohio—see the Frogman chapter in my book *Southern Ohio Legends & Lore* and the Grassman chapter in *Central Ohio Legends & Lore*. And in Northern Ohio, it happened to Orange Eyes.

To unpack all this, we should start with the popular version of the Orange Eyes legend. The creature is described as Bigfoot-like: big, tall and hairy. Some reports have the creature standing eleven feet tall and weighing one

Riverside Cemetery, the alleged former residence of Orange Eyes. *Photo courtesy of Wendy Cywinski.*

thousand pounds. And of course, there are the glowing orange eyes from which the creature gets its name. It's said that Orange Eyes was first spotted in 1959, when it was living "in the sewers of Riverside Cemetery," but construction and development forced the creature south. Today, Orange Eyes is said to hang out around the various Lovers Lanes near Charles Mill Lake, especially off Ruggles Road.

So there's lots to unpack here. To sort through this, let's start with the sighting of Orange Eyes that offers the most specific information: the 1959 sighting. We are given a particular date for this sighting: March 28, 1959. We also have an exact location—sort of. Most versions describe it as a "desolate stretch of country road" known locally as Lovers Lane. Other versions claim the Lovers Lane is officially known as Ruggles Road, which "runs along the Charles Mill reservoir." In all versions, three teenagers encounter a giant, hairy creature with glowing orange eyes.

Even a cursory glance at this legend will reveal that it is just a retelling of the Charles Mill Lake Monster encounter (see the "Thing from Charles Mill Lake" chapter in this book). As evidence, I submit the date the event is said to have happened: March 28, 1959. While the Charles Mill Lake encounter happened on March 26, 1959, it's clearly the same event. The March 28 date comes from the fact that the local newspaper, the *News Journal*, first printed the Charles Mill Lake story on March 28. Oddly enough, the article's headline was "Boys Report Seeing Green-Eyed Monster," so while the eye color is wrong, the fact that the monster's eyes are mentioned could have been why these stories merged. Three teens were involved in the Charles Mill Lake incident, which checks out. But they were parked at the water's edge, not on a Lovers Lane or a Ruggles Road. So where did those tidbits of information come from? For that, we must move forward a few years to 1968, when there were "a lot" of Orange Eyes sightings.

During the summer of 1968, teenagers in and around Norwalk, Ohio, sometimes ventured out to an old road off Ruggles Road, which they called

Lovers Lane. On certain nights, usually around eleven thirty, glowing orange eyes could be seen in and around the woods. The eyes would appear to grow, shrink and move around the woods, often ending up near an abandoned old house next to a bridge.

You see things coming together, don't you? We now have Ruggles Road, the Lovers Lane and even glowing orange eyes. One big problem: the 1968 sightings took place in Norwalk, Ohio, about forty miles north of Charles Mill Lake, and if we're trying to connect all the dots, Norwalk is over ninety miles west of Cleveland's Riverside Cemetery, where Orange Eyes was said to live. There is also the inescapable fact that in November 1968, the Huron County Sheriff's Department "captured" Orange Eyes, which wasn't a monster.

The November 19, 1968 edition of the *Norwalk Reflector* ran an article under the headline "'Orange Eyes' Mystery Solved." The article mentions the story of Orange Eyes and the fact that the summer before, teens hanging out on Ruggles Road swore they would sometimes see a pair of orange eyes staring out at them from the woods near "the old bridge." Local police had heard the stories about Orange Eyes but thought it was just teens playing harmless pranks on each other. But then they started getting reports of vandalism at the abandoned house on Ruggles Road and decided to investigate.

According to the article, when the police arrived at the abandoned house, they found it had been vandalized. They also found a handwritten note on a small stand inside the house: "We were here, Orange Eyes, and we will return tonight." As the officers stood inside the house, they noticed something strange out in the woods: a pair of glowing orange eyes that seemed to be changing shape, as if they were moving. They moved in closer, and, according to the article, this is what they found:

> *A pair of orange reflectors were hung from two small trees near the bridge. On moonlit nights, the light would shine on them, and the reflection made it appear two orange eyes were staring out of the woods. Breezes would blow the reflectors, making them appear to shrink and grow. Apparently, someone would come back and take the reflectors down, then put them back up to scare another victim.*

The sheriff's department removed the reflectors, and that appears to have been the end of Orange Eyes, as there were no more reports in the area. The creator of Orange Eyes was never identified.

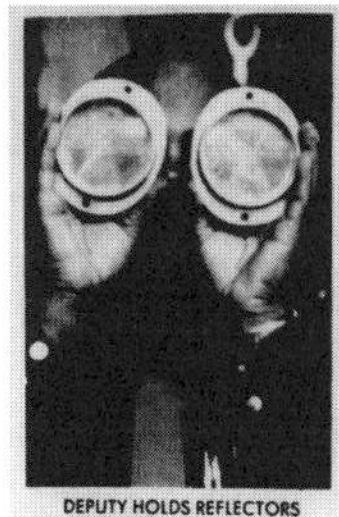

DEPUTY HOLDS REFLECTORS
He Is Sgt. Leslie Harper

'Orange Eyes' Mystery Solved

It was a breezy, moonlit night. The youth had taken his girlfriend to the Ruggles Bridge, on Ruggles Road, north of Norwalk.

It's a spot young lovers often frequent.

In the woods off the bridge they saw a pair of orange eyes staring at them. Their romantic mood turned to fear.

The young couple may have been the first to see "Orange Eyes," a mystery that haunted young lovers all summer long.

In an abandoned house near the bridge, a note was found on a small stand. On it a message was scrawled: "WE WERE HERE, ORANGE EYES, AND WE WILL RETURN TONIGHT."

Many reported seeing the strange pair of eyes in the woods, about 20 feet from the bridge.

A brave young man would take his best girl there so that "Orange Eyes" might entice her to snuggle.

"Orange Eyes" would usually come out around 11:30 p.m. Sometimes the eyes seemed to grow and shrink, they said.

The Huron County Sheriff's Department solved the mystery of "Orange Eyes" Nov. 10 while investigating vandalism of the abandoned house, said Deputy John Warner. The story wasn't made public until Monday.

A pair of orange reflectors were hung from two small trees near the bridge. On moonlit nights, the light would shine on them and the reflection made it appear two orange eyes were staring out of the woods.

Breezes would blow the reflectors making them appear to shrink and grow.

Apparently someone would come back and take the reflectors down then put them back up to scare another victim.

The Sheriff's Department thinks there is some connection between the vandalism and "Orange Eyes." It believes several persons are involved.

Sheriff John Borgia said the whole idea may have started as a prank but when the vandalism started, he felt the whole idea was no longer a prank.

What furniture was left in the house was defaced and someone had written on the walls.

The creator of "Orange Eyes" is still unknown.

Above: The only newspaper article to show Orange Eyes after his capture by the Huron County Sheriff's Department. *From* The Norwalk Reflector, *Tuesday, November 19, 1968.*

Left: Try as we might, we could find no sign of Orange Eyes in any of Riverside Cemetery's sewers. *Photo courtesy of Wendy Cywinski.*

The only aspect of Orange Eyes that we've yet to touch on is the account of the creature having Bigfoot-like characteristics. For that, we can look back to the early 1970s, specifically 1972, a big year for Bigfoot sightings in Ohio. In 1972, there were Bigfoot sightings across the state, as far south as Gallia County and as far north as Toledo and even "at a cemetery outside Cleveland." These sightings all involved creatures that were described as big and hairy. The same can't be said for the 1972 sightings outside of Ohio. In July 1972, residents of Missouri went out looking for a creature that became known as Momo (Missouri Monster). Momo was described as being seven feet tall and covered in black fur, with a pumpkin-shaped head and glowing orange eyes.

The moral of this story is: Don't be so quick to throw all creature sightings together. The result can be that one-off creatures like the Charles Mill Lake Monster and some version of what would become Orange Eyes can inadvertently get lost to time. We can't let that happen.

CHAPTER 4
SLITHERING THROUGH PENINSULA

Nestled in the heart of Cuyahoga Valley National Park is Peninsula, Ohio, a small village with a big personality. Some say that something even bigger lurks in the village: the Peninsula Python, rumored to have terrorized Peninsula and the surrounding area during the summer of 1944.

According to the Peninsula Historical Society, the first documented incident occurred on June 8, 1944. Several days before the sighting, farmer Clarence Mitchell said his dogs started acting funny, especially when he tried to get them to go into his cornfield with him. Eventually, the dogs refused to go anywhere near the cornfield. On June 8, Mitchell was working in the field when something made him look up, and he saw, about fifteen feet away, "the biggest snake I ever see [*sic*]." Mitchell said he watched the snake for several minutes until it slithered down to the Cuyahoga River, swam across and then came out the other side, disappearing into the brush. When he was asked to describe the snake, Mitchell said:

> *He was thick as my thigh, right here, and every bit of fifteen feet long—more like eighteen—sort of brownish spotted. I went over and looked at the track. It was like you'd rolled a spare tire across my field.*

Nearby, Mike Bobacek was working east of the river when he saw Clarence Mitchell running across his field toward his house. As he watched Mitchell, movement near the river's edge caught Bobacek's eye. Bobacek said he saw a giant snake emerge from the river and head east.

Ten days later, on June 18, John and Paul Szalay returned from lunch to the field they'd been working in, a few miles north of where Clarence Mitchell had seen the snake. The pair found a weird track in the dirt, "like from an auto tire," which stretched from the field down to the river, where it disappeared. Now here's where things get interesting: the two men decide to make Mayor John Rich aware of the strange track. Not only was Mayor Rich interested, but he also decided to go out to the field and see the track himself, and he brought Police Chief Art Huey and two assistant chiefs, Dale Hall and Dud Watson, along. After viewing the tracks, Mayor Rich issued an official statement: "Nothing but a mighty big snake could've made that track."

Now, when the mayor claims there is a giant snake in town, real or imagined, people will start seeing said snake everywhere. In 1944 Peninsula, it only took two days. Mrs. Roy Vaughn looked out of the second floor of her henhouse into the backyard and saw "a great big snake trying to get through the woven wire fence." The snake was having trouble fitting through the fence because it "had a lump in him, big as a basket." As she watched, the snake reared up and climbed over the fence, which was almost four feet high, and down the other side. With the snake gone, Mrs. Vaughn ran down to where she had last seen it and noticed that one of her chickens was missing. The snake had made off with it. Not sure what to do next, Mrs. Vaughn contacted the fire department, who alerted Mayor Rich. After visiting the scene, the mayor announced that a giant snake, possibly a python, was loose in Peninsula. In an attempt to capture said snake, Mayor Rich tasked Chief Huey with organizing a snake hunt, set to take place the coming Sunday, June 25, at ten o'clock in the morning.

The June 26 edition of the *Akron Beacon Journal* featured an article by Rayy Mitten chronicling the snake hunt that had taken place in Peninsula the previous day. Mitten arrived in Peninsula at ten o'clock, the appointed time for the start of the hunt. The proceedings began with a short lecture "on safety in snake hunting by Police Chief Art Huey." Huey then told the group that Mayor John Rich had ordered only group leaders to carry firearms. Everyone was broken into groups, and those who were not allowed to have firearms picked up "hunting knives, butcher knives, tree limbs, ropes and various other non-lethal weapons." Then, about sixty snake hunters went into the woods, hoping to find and capture the snake. At the end of the day, Mitten was left to conclude that the only thing the searchers found was "how sore unused muscles can get." Someone had reported seeing the snake and sounded the alarm, but that was determined to have been a hoax.

DEATH SENTENCE HAS BEEN DECREED FOR 'PENINSULA PYTHON'

Left: When posses were formed to find the Peninsula Python, they clearly weren't playing. *From* The Daily Advocate, *Wednesday, June 28, 1944.*

Below: When the people of Peninsula were unable to locate the python, some came to believe it had slithered on to a new town. *From* The Evening Independent, *Saturday, July 15, 1944.*

Peninsula's Python Here; So Say West End Residents

Ladies and gentlemen, the biggest snake outside captivity is in the West Brookfield section of Massillon. (Believe it or not).

The "Peninsula python" has left its Summit county haunts, crawling away from the snake hunting posses, to find haven in the west end of Massillon.

That's what some residents of the west end of the city are saying. Some however modify the conclusion that the snake is the "Peninsula python," but almost simultaneously add that it's just as big.

As yet no snake-hunting posse has been organized but Police Capt. Royal E. Smith, himself a resident of the west end, says residents there no longer are taking short cuts through the fields. Mothers have cautioned their children not to wander away from their homes for fear of the python, says the police officer.

And state highway patrolmen today say they have received many telephone calls in the last few days from excited persons inquring about the snake.

Like Massillon police the state patrolmen have not taken the snake story seriously.

Some might have thought the unsuccessful snake hunt meant the creature had slithered away, if it ever existed. But clearly, it was just lying low, because two days later, on June 27, Pauline Hopko was heading out to milk her cows when she heard crashing sounds in the branches of a willow tree on the other side of the Cuyahoga River. She then saw a snake "with a head as big as a man's coming down out of that dead willow." On Thursday, June 29, Ernest Raymond was mowing his fencerow near Brandywine Creek when he noticed a "stump" start to uncoil and lift its head. Raymond ran back to his house to get his shotgun, but when he returned, the snake had lowered his head, and it quickly disappeared into the tall grass before Raymond could get a shot off.

Back at the offices of the *Akron Beacon Journal*, reporter Rayy Mitten, never one to give up on a story easily, came up with a way to capture irrefutable evidence of the giant snake. On July 1, Mitten went to the Sky-Haven Airport near Macedonia, Ohio, and got pilot Slim Honroth to take him up in a Piper Cub plane to search for the giant snake from above. Armed with binoculars, Mitten scanned the ground below. The small plane crisscrossed back and forth over Peninsula, passing several times over Ernest Raymond's property, scene of the latest snake sighting. Once again, Mitten came away empty-handed.

Back in Peninsula, an unofficial python posse was formed, consisting primarily of volunteers who would respond "immediately" to the scene of any reported snake sighting. The problem was that once a sighting was reported, it took them several hours to get on scene, by which time the snake was long gone. There were a few more sightings through the summer of 1944 and into the fall. As news of the Peninsula Python spread across Ohio, the United States and, finally, the world, the village was overrun with snake hunters. Eventually, with nothing to go on, even the snake hunters left, and things went back to normal.

So did the Peninsula Python ever exist? And if so, where did it come from? Most who believe in the snake will say it escaped from a traveling circus that had been in Akron, less than twenty miles away, about a month before the sightings began. Authorities tracked down the circus, which stated that all its snakes were accounted for. Skeptics still held on to the idea that the snake came from that circus, which only said it didn't because it didn't want to be held liable for any damage the snake did.

Others said that while the snake came from a circus, it wasn't the circus that had been in Akron. Instead, they pointed to a carnival truck crash in the area about two years ago. The driver was killed, and the truck's contents spilled across the region. Maybe the snake came from that crash.

Wildlife experts, however, are not so sure. While pythons can certainly grow to the length that the citizens of Peninsula were reporting, they are not native to Ohio. Even if such a snake were released in Ohio, it would not be able to stay alive very long in Ohio's climate. But again, those who believe in the snake's existence will say that's why the reports of the snake stopped in the fall: the snake died.

While the snake might have died, its legend certainly didn't. Stories of the Peninsula Python still exist, especially on the Internet, where they grow, as does the snake's length—some sites claim it's over thirty feet long. Even Peninsula, Ohio, got in on the act when the Peninsula Village Council made the python its official mascot. They've even been known to host a Peninsula Python Parade, complete with a hundred-foot-long python modeled after Chinese dragon parade costumes. The Peninsula Python takes fourteen people to operate.

PART VI

LEGENDARY EVENTS

CHAPTER 1

THE ASHTABULA TRAIN DISASTER

On the morning of December 25, 1876, children and adults alike sprang from their beds to take in the spectacle and majesty of a white Christmas. It's been said that all Christmas Day, the festivities were jollier, the carolers sang louder and the holidays candles glowed just a bit brighter. Of course, when the snow had yet to stop the following morning, that all changed. Roads were impassable, and people were already tired of shoveling. The snow continued for another day before it looked like the weather was starting to clear. However, on the morning of Friday, December 29, weather forecasters were calling for even more snow, coupled with heavy winds. Severe winds. Commuters hopped onto trains and made their way to work, hoping the forecast was wrong and there'd be no more snow. They couldn't have been more wrong. By the afternoon of December 29, over two feet of snow blanketed Northern Ohio, and the wind gusts were tracked at over fifty miles per hour. These were the weather conditions that the No. 5 Pacific Express train was attempting to navigate through.

The No. 5 Pacific Express was a regular and had traveled many times from Erie, Pennsylvania, to Ashtabula, Ohio, but never in these conditions. The tracks were covered in snow and ice, forcing the train to go slower than usual and, in some cases, stop altogether to clear the tracks. As a result, the train was two hours overdue for its 5:00 p.m. arrival time in Ashtabula. On this particular journey, the No. 5 consisted of eleven passenger cars and two locomotives: the *Socrates*, the lead locomotive, and the *Columbia*. There were approximately 160 crew members and passengers onboard, including engineer Daniel McGuire, who was operating the *Socrates*.

At approximately 7:25 p.m., McGuire saw a familiar sight: the massive 154-foot-long bridge spanning the Ashtabula River, over 70 feet in the air. To McGuire, it meant that this leg of the journey was nearing an end, because the Ashtabula train depot was on the other side of the bridge. There was only one problem: the tracks ahead were covered in snow. McGuire didn't want to risk his train getting stuck in the snow halfway across the bridge, so he decided to speed up, hoping the *Socrates*'s engine would knock the snow from the tracks as it rumbled across. It worked: the *Socrates* made quick work of the snow. But as the locomotive reached the bridge's western side, it began to slow down. Initially believing this was because the train was climbing a steep hill near the depot, McGuire would later say, he peeked out the *Socrates*'s window and looked back at the rest of the train. That's when he saw that the bridge was starting to collapse.

McGuire knew he had to act quickly, so he opened the throttle on the *Socrates*, hoping to outrun the falling bridge and get the entire train to the western bank. The *Socrates* did not respond immediately; it shook violently several times before lurching forward and continuing across the bridge. It was believed that the shaking of the locomotive caused *Socrates* to uncouple from the rest of the train. This was good news for McGuire: as the *Socrates*'s load was now significantly reduced, it could make it across the bridge and onto the tracks on the western side. Unfortunately, this meant that the rest of the train, including the second locomotive, the *Columbia*, was now sitting stranded in the middle of the bridge, which was collapsing behind the train.

As soon as he could bring the *Socrates* to a complete stop, McGuire jumped from the locomotive and ran back to the bridge to see what he could do to help. But the bridge was gone, as was the rest of the No. 5 Pacific Express. It was all at the bottom of a snow-covered ravine near the Ashtabula River. McGuire called down but heard no one respond. All was silent. Knowing he couldn't climb down the ravine by himself, McGuire turned and ran down the tracks to the Ashtabula Depot and sounded the alarm. As telegraphs were feverishly sent out to shut down the tracks, McGuire gathered everyone he could, and they made their way back to the remains of the bridge. The group was horrified to find the train wreckage engulfed in flames. It would later be determined that most people onboard the train had survived the initial fall from the bridge. But as the cars landed, they started stacking up, one on top of the other, resulting in a massive pile of wood and metal. The bridge was composed mainly of wood, and that debris added to the pile. It is believed that the overturned kerosene lamps in the passenger cars fueled the fire and allowed it to spread quickly. To make matters even worse, the heat from the fire caused the ice on the Ashtabula River to crack, forcing the survivors to contend with fire and water on top of the bitter cold.

Somehow, Daniel McGuire and the small group of men he had gathered managed to climb down the embankment, and they tried to pull people from the wreckage. They were joined by people who lived near the bridge and had heard the crash. The Ashtabula Fire Department arrived and dragged their water hoses down to extinguish the flames. When it became apparent that their efforts would be futile and that the wreckage was in danger of falling into the river, the decision was made to stop trying to put the fire out and instead rescue as many victims as possible. Try as they might, they could save only a few people before the flames became unbearable. After the first few minutes, they were unable to rescue any survivors. The fire would be left to burn itself out, hours later.

The following morning, authorities started the process of removing all the victims from the wreckage and trying to identify them. Needless to say, it was a long and tedious process, as most of the bodies were burned beyond recognition. The remains were removed from the crash site and brought to a freight depot, where they were laid out alongside any personal items that may have been found nearby. A mass viewing was then held for family members in the hopes that all the crash victims could be identified.

Entrance to Chestnut Grove Cemetery, where some of the victims of the Ashtabula train disaster are buried. *Author photo.*

Left: Memorial to the victims of the Ashtabula bridge disaster at Chestnut Grove Cemetery. *Author photo.*

Below: The base of the Unrecognized Dead memorial at Chestnut Grove Cemetery. *Author photo.*

Right: Mausoleum of Charles Collins, one of the engineers who worked on the ill-fated Ashtabula train bridge. *Author photo.*

Below: Legend has it that in photos, Collins's mausoleum always appears "burned" due to his involvement in the train disaster. *Author photo.*

Official passenger records were also consulted to try to help with identification. That ended up being problematic, as those records did not match the head count on the train. Regardless, it was established that the crash had taken the lives of eighty-nine people. Sixty-three others had been injured (five of whom would later pass away as a result of their injuries). At the time, the Ashtabula train disaster was the worst train wreck in United States history, and so it remained until the Great Train Wreck of 1918 in Nashville, Tennessee. Today, it stands as the third-deadliest rail accident in United States history.

At the end of the mass viewing, while many of the bodies had been claimed by family members, there were nineteen that were never identified, as well as partial remains. Those were taken to Ashtabula's Chestnut Grove Cemetery, where a special service was held on January 19, 1877, and the victims were laid to rest in a mass grave, in the shadow of a thirty-seven-foot-tall stone obelisk that marks their final resting place. Oddly enough, this monument is next to the mausoleum of another individual involved in the incident: Charles Collins.

Collins was in charge of inspecting the collapsed bridge. During an inquest, he stated that he had checked the bridge only ten days before the crash and found it structurally sound. However, a special inquest into the accident disagreed and presented evidence showing that the bridge's supports had been continually shifting and were almost three inches out of alignment at the time of the collapse. This must have significantly affected Collins, as after hearing that testimony, he went home and committed suicide.

The fact that Collins chose to take his own life over a train disaster and that his final resting place faces a memorial to that disaster has naturally given rise to stories that Charles Collins's ghost haunts the cemetery. Collins's mausoleum always appears "burned" in photographs, and his ghost is also seen, head bowed, standing in front of the train disaster memorial. More often than not, however, his ghost is seen sitting on the steps of his mausoleum. He never interacts with anyone and buries his head in his hands, crying and softly saying, "I'm sorry. I'm sorry."

CHAPTER 2

CALLING MICHAEL JACKSON

To my teenage daughter, there are so many things in this world that "always were." They've never not existed in her world. So she can't comprehend that strange stories would emerge from things that have always been real. Case in point: barcodes. In my daughter's world, they are everywhere. In fact, between barcodes and QR codes, my daughter scans all sorts of things. It's second nature to her. But barcodes weren't always a thing, and when they started showing up on things in the mid-1970s, people were confused about what their purpose was. Some believed they were secret coded messages that only a select few could interpret and understand. Fair enough. But how and why did people start believing that Michael Jackson had hidden his home phone number in the barcode of one of the most popular albums of all time? Well, that's a different topic altogether!

What's commonly referred as a barcode is actually a universal product code (UPC). A UPC is a standardized way of tracking specific items for inventory purposes. Each item is given the same unique UPC so companies can tell how many are being sold and how many remain in inventory. While UPCs had existed since the early 1970s, and Wrigley's Chewing Gum started putting them on their products in 1974, it hadn't gotten to the point where consumers could scan them themselves or knew what they were. They didn't hit the mainstream until the 1980s.

In popular music, most point to Elvis Costello's 1979 release *Armed Forces* as the first album to include a UPC. Other record companies followed suit, and by the early 1980s, more and more new releases featured UPCs on them.

Companies even started adding UPCs to reissued albums released before 1979, resulting in some copies of the same album having UPCs and others not. But let's not forget, this was the 1980s, when everyone was putting their record albums under a microscope in search of weird symbols and hidden meanings. Just the sight of these new UPCs and their strange collection of bars and numbers screamed that there must be some secret, nefarious reason behind their very existence.

Michael Jackson released the album *Thriller* on November 29, 1982. To say that *Thriller* impacted popular music would be a gross understatement. The album spent thirty-seven weeks at No. 1 on the Billboard charts. Seven of the album's nine tracks were released as singles. All of them reached at least the Top 10 of the Hot 100, and two, "Beat It" and "Billie Jean," reached No. 1. To date, the album has sold over seventy million copies worldwide, making it the best-selling album of all time. That meant there were a lot of copies of *Thriller* out there in the wild—copies with a mysterious bar-looking thing on them. It had to mean something, right? But what? And that's when Barbara Brown's phone started ringing off the hook.

Who's Barbara Brown? In the 1980s, she was a nurse living in Youngstown, Ohio, with an unlisted phone number. One night, her phone rang. When Barbara answered it, the voice on the other end sheepishly asked, "Is Michael Jackson there?" After telling the caller they had the wrong number and hanging up, Barbara shrugged it off, until the phone rang again—and again. All the callers were looking to talk to Michael Jackson. As the phone continued to ring off the hook, Barbara was able to start piecing together why everyone was calling. It appeared a rumor had started that a phone number was hidden within the UPC on *Thriller*—the number to Michael Jackson's home residence.

At first, Barbara tried to ignore the calls, but at the height of the craze, she received up to a dozen of them daily. What's worse, some callers believed they were ringing up Michael Jackson's home in California, so they would adjust when they called to Pacific Standard Time—meaning they were calling Ohio in the middle of the night. When the callers began to get more persistent, often accusing Barbara of lying and insisting that Michael Jackson really was there, she started quizzing them about how they managed to get her number. She was told the secret was dialing "1-800" and then the first seven digits of the UPC. Others said the phone number was scrambled within the UPC and that they needed to unscramble it for the correct number to appear. Either way, the phone calls continued, seemingly with no end in sight.

Back cover of Michael Jackson's *Thriller*, featuring the notorious barcode. *Author photo.*

Frustrated, Barbara contacted the phone company, which told her to change her number. Barbara was unwilling to do that because, in her words, "It's my number, not Michael Jackson's." She next reached out to the local media, including radio stations. She even suggested to the radio stations that before they played a Michael Jackson song, they could tell listeners that Jackson's home number wasn't hidden on the *Thriller* album and to please stop calling. "They just laughed at me," Barbara told reporters. As for the news articles, they only served to entice more people to call, convinced that Jackson's number was hidden on the album and all the previous callers didn't use the right "formula" to reveal it. The one good thing that came out of the newspaper articles was that reporters then turned to Michael Jackson's team and *Thriller*'s record label, Epic, and its mothership, CBS Records. They all denied any connection between the album's barcode and a phone number; the UPC, they said, was just a way to track sales and inventory.

In the end, things began to die down, and Barbara's phone stopped ringing as much. Those who did call were looking to speak with Barbara or a member of her family, not Michael Jackson. So how did this happen? As discussed, the UPCs themselves, being something new, were partly responsible, as they gave people who were already scouring albums for secret clues something new to ponder. This ties into the popular obsession with the idea that there are secrets and hidden meanings to be found in everyday objects.

Regarding the need to call "1-800" before the numbers in the UPC, on June 29, 1984, a series of print ads began running in newspapers and magazines across the United States that listed a phone number to call to "hear Michael Jackson." The number in the ads was one that hadn't been seen before: "Call 1-900..." The rest of the phone number in the ads contained digits that also appeared in the *Thriller* UPC, albeit in a different order. So the possibility exists that the *Thriller* UPC urban legend and the very real 1-900 number merged into one.

If nothing else, this story ties into the age-old desire to connect with our heroes. The pull to get invited into a celebrity's inner circle can be immense and still exists today. Yes, the idea that Michael Jackson would hide his home number on the back of one of his records seems far-fetched, but if it only costs the price of a phone call to find out, what's the harm?

CHAPTER 3

THE RETURN OF THE HINCKLEY BUZZARDS

Over the years, Ohio has been home to quite a few weird festivals: the Moonshine Festival in New Straitsville, North Ridgeville's SkunkFest and even the Washboard Music Fest in Logan. But perhaps one of the strangest involves people everywhere waking up on March 15, grabbing a pair of binoculars and heading to Hinckley, Ohio, to watch the skies for approaching buzzards.

While Buzzard Day is officially March 15, the annual celebration takes place—and has been taking place since 1957—on the first Sunday after March 15, if the fifteenth doesn't fall on a Sunday. Buzzard Day always kicks off with Hinckley hosting a pancake breakfast. From there, visitors are welcome to wander through the craft fair, play some games, maybe even get their faces painted. Then it's just a short walk to Hinckley Reservation, the third-largest Cleveland Metroparks reservation, coming in at a whopping 3,200 acres. Once inside the reservation, you'll want to go up to the Buzzard Roost, because that's where all the action is. If you're lucky enough, you can grab a spot along the fence line, where you can stare out across the fields, looking for a familiar dark shape to appear on the horizon. If you see one, yell it out, because if it is a buzzard, your sighting will get added to the official tally board for all to see. Of course, there is a slight problem that no one seems to care about: the birds everyone is waiting to see return, the ones Buzzard Day is named after, aren't buzzards at all. They are turkey vultures.

Left: Hinckley Township, where all buzzards are welcome. *Author photo.*

Below: For the best chance of witnessing the buzzards' return, make your way to the Buzzard Roost. *Author photo.*

Like I mentioned, no one seems to care what you call the creatures that allegedly come swarming back to Hinckley, Ohio, every year almost like clockwork. But there is a marked difference between buzzards and turkey vultures, which might aid in determining which version of how all this got started might be closer to the truth. Buzzards eat living creatures, while turkey vultures are more like the animal kingdom's sanitation engineers: they "clean up" deceased creatures. If you're still having trouble figuring out the difference, the next time you drive through Ohio and see a large black bird feasting on roadkill, you're looking at a turkey vulture.

So how does what a turkey vulture eats help us identify the origin story? To answer that question, we must go back to 1795, when Judge Samuel Hinckley of Northampton, Massachusetts, purchased what would become Hinckley Township from the Connecticut Land Company for the whopping price of twenty-three cents an acre. Judge Hinckley purchased the area more as an investment than a place where he could live. His thought was that with people looking to push out from the East and settle out West, all he had to do was sit on the land and wait for its value to go up. So those purchasing property in Hinckley were on their own. This meant that much of the area around Hinckley remained wooded and full of wildlife—some would say too much wildlife, because some of the settlers found most of their livestock killed by wolves and their crops being destroyed or eaten by area bears and wolves. All this gave rise to the legend of the Great Hinckley Hunt of 1818.

If the stories are to be believed, in the fall of 1818, the residents had had enough and decided something needed to be done about the wildlife living around Hinckley. They needed to protect their families, livestock and crops. That's when they determined that a "war of extermination" was required. The plan was to send invitations to every man and boy in the area, inviting them out for a special hunt. Shortly before Christmas, everyone was to gather in a long, wide semicircle with any weapons they could find and move forward, driving all the wolves and bears they came across ahead of them until they were backed into a confined area near some cliffs where they couldn't escape. And then, well, the extermination would take place.

This story has been passed down through history and is always vague in its specifics, including the names of the people who participated. However, it is said that on the day of the extermination, close to six hundred men and boys showed up, armed with everything from guns and pistols to clubs and spears. By the end of the hunt, it is said that seventeen wolves, twenty-one bears and three hundred deer had been killed. All that meat made for quite

the celebration as everyone in and around Hinckley came to the center of the town to partake in the Christmas feast.

How does all this tie into the Hinckley buzzards? Well, if you believe that this hunt/extermination took place, it is what brought the buzzards to Hinckley in the first place. Remember, the buzzards are actually turkey vultures that like to feed on dead animals. So the idea that the 1818 event resulted in an enormous number of carcasses that attracted the buzzards' attention, so much so that they were drawn back to the area year after year, is intriguing. But you have to consider that the 1818 event is alleged to have happened in December, a good three months before the buzzards would start showing up. Sure, you could claim that there were a lot of animals killed that year, meaning a lot of carcasses left to decay. But the counter to that is that these settlers had to withstand a cold winter while fending off bears and wolves, so they were not wasting any part of the animals they killed. Come March the following year, there probably wasn't much left to draw the buzzards in.

More than likely, the buzzards were attracted by the Hinckley area's terrain. Hinckley Reservation is a perfect area for turkey vultures to hang out in. Not only is it home to the ninety-acre Hinckley Lake, but it is also heavily wooded, and there are multiple rocky ledges throughout the reservation. A

Opposite: Once your buzzard sighting is confirmed, it gets added to the official Buzzard Scoreboard. *Author photo.*

Above: Yours truly, scanning the horizon for buzzards. *Photo courtesy of Stephanie D. Willis.*

little-known fact about turkey vultures is that they don't nest like other birds. They prefer to roost, like chickens. So the plethora of trees and rocky ledges make for perfect roosting spots.

Another important fact is that while the mass hunt took place in 1818, well over one hundred years passed before people started noticing that buzzards were hanging around Hinckley. In fact, the first Buzzard Day wasn't celebrated until 1957. But in the end, does any of this matter? Ohioans have never been shy about finding an excuse to have a good time. So if all it takes to get you out of the house and walking in nature is a pancake breakfast, some arts and crafts and a chance to be the first to spot a turkey vulture coming in for a landing at Buzzard Roost, so be it.

CHAPTER 4

THE GREAT UFO CHASE OF 1966

One of the strangest unexplained UFO incidents began early on Sunday, April 17, 1966. Portage County Deputies Dale Spaur, thirty-five, and Wilbur L. "Barney" Neff, twenty-six, were on routine patrol in Car P-13, and so far, their shift had been uneventful. At approximately five o'clock in the morning, the deputies were heading west on US Route 224 toward Randolph, Ohio, when they saw a vehicle, a white 1959 Ford, parked on the southern shoulder, just east of Randolph proper. Spaur, who was driving, turned the cruiser around and parked. Both deputies exited the vehicle, and as Spaur began to approach the vehicle, Neff stayed with the police car.

Spaur reached the vehicle and called back to Neff to say that it was empty. Spaur then began scanning the woods to see if he could locate a driver. Spaur would later say it was at this time that he first noticed the bright light in the sky. It was on the southern side of Route 224 and appeared to be moving eastward toward the deputies. Spaur would later say that the object was only about one hundred feet off the ground, barely clearing the trees as it moved closer. Spaur thought it was a plane in distress but noted that the object gave off only a low humming sound.

As the object got closer, Spaur yelled for Neff to look behind him. Neff looked over his right shoulder and, for the first time, saw the object himself. As the two deputies stared at the object, it suddenly stopped for a moment, as if it realized it was being observed, before again advancing on the officers. Since the object appeared wider than the road, Spaur estimated it to be between thirty-five and forty-five feet wide, maybe even fifty, and between fifteen and twenty-five feet tall. It was shaped "like the head of a flashlight," and there was a bright beam of blue-white light, like that from an arc welder, coming from the bottom of the object. This light illuminated the ground below and was so bright that Spaur and Neff could not look directly at it. Still, the only sound was a low, steady hum, like from high-tension power lines.

While the two officers stood there, transfixed, the object crossed the highway directly above them. That's when Spaur and Neff decided they would be safer inside their cruiser. Once inside the car, unsure what to do next, they watched as the object paused on the northern side of Route 224 and started heading back toward their car. Spaur radioed in that an unknown object was directly over their patrol car. Radio operator Deputy Robert Wilson responded to Spaur and noted that Spaur called in at 5:07 a.m. The craft crossed over the police cruiser, continued north and then moved three hundred feet to the east before stopping again, hovering just above the treetops.

When Deputy Wilson was told that the object had stopped again and was just hovering there, he asked Spaur if he thought he could hit it if he shot at it. As Spaur considered the possibility of firing on the object, Sergeant Hank Shoenfelt got on the line and asked if Spaur or Neff had a camera with them. Spaur responded, "No," and Shoenfelt said he'd work on getting an officer with a camera out there.

As all the officers contemplated their next steps, the object started moving eastward. When Spaur informed the station, Shoenfelt told him to follow it and keep it in sight so they could identify it. Spaur put the cruiser in drive, and off they went.

As the object moved east, it started picking up speed, but oddly enough, it kept following Route 224, which made it somewhat easy for Spaur to keep following it. At one point, Spaur reported that he was driving over eighty miles an hour to keep pace with it. But he noticed that when he had to slow down, the object seemed to slow down, too, as if it was waiting for the cruiser to catch back up. Spaur also said that while the object moved from the north side of the road to the south side (and sometimes directly overhead), it never made any quick or sudden movements as if it was trying to shake the police cruiser.

As they traveled, Neff found he had to almost press his face against the windshield to see the object. Still, he could tell that it was egg-shaped and seemed to have what looked like an antenna toward the back. The beam of light stayed focused on the ground, even when the object rose to about three hundred feet in the air.

At some point, while continuing east, Spaur and Neff got off Route 224 and onto Route 14. We know this happened because East Palestine Police Department Patrolman Wayne Huston, thirty-two, heard the radio chatter about Spaur chasing a strange object in the sky and decided he wanted in on it. Huston drove his patrol car, OV-1, to the intersection of Routes 14 and 170 and waited.

Huston would later say that he first saw the object when it was about five miles away, moving toward his patrol car from the west. Huston estimated the object's altitude to be between eight hundred and nine hundred feet. The skies were clear, so Huston was able to get a good look at the object. He stated that it looked like a "melted ice cream cone" and the "cone" portion looked like the beam of a flashlight. Huston did not report hearing any sound coming from the object. As it flew past his car, Huston estimated it was moving at eighty to eighty-five miles per hour.

As soon as the object passed in front of him, Huston could see the police lights from Spaur's cruiser approaching and hear the siren. As soon as Spaur passed, Huston turned on his lights and siren and joined in the chase.

Before long, the object and the police cars crossed the Ohio-Pennsylvania line, entering Beaver County, Pennsylvania. While continuing straight, Ohio Route 14 had turned into Pennsylvania Route 51. Spaur, unfamiliar with Pennsylvania roads and losing his connection to his Ohio office, was now driving somewhat blind. Huston, who patrolled close to the Pennsylvania border and was somewhat familiar with the roads, at least close to the border, was calling out directions to Spaur over the radio. But they were also trying to put the word out for a Pennsylvania officer to come and take the lead on the pursuit.

The object led the patrol cars into Rochester, Pennsylvania, where it continued moving towards the east. As the officers were now driving on unfamiliar back roads through hilly terrain, they had to slow down, which caused them to start falling behind the object. Additionally, the object was simply moving east, not necessarily following a known road. This meant the officers often had to turn down side streets and cut-throughs to continue following the eastern route the object was taking. Before too long, the officers lost sight of the object. Incredibly, as the officers crested a hill, the object appeared right in front of them, hovering as if waiting for them to catch up.

As they continued the chase through Freedom, Pennsylvania, and into Conway, Spaur noticed he was getting low on gas. Seeing an Atlantic gas station ahead on Route 65, he pulled into the parking lot. Huston followed suit. That's when they saw Conway Patrolman Frank Panzanella standing outside his cruiser in the gas station parking lot, watching the object.

Oddly enough, while Panzanella had been watching the object for the past thirty minutes, he wasn't aware there had been a chase. His first indication of this was when the two cruisers pulled into the gas station. Panzanella said that the object he observed was unlike any known aircraft he had ever seen before. What he saw looked like "half a football," between twenty-five and thirty feet across. It was moving approximately one thousand feet above the ground.

Sheriff Chases UFO 86 Miles

RAVENNA, Ohio (AP)—"We were close, closer than I ever want to be again," said a deputy sheriff who chased an unidentified flying object from Ohio into Pennsylvania.

Portage County Deputy Sheriff Dale Spaur said he and his partner, W.L. Neff, "were close" to the object in separate cars and chased it 86 miles for an hour and a half, from near Ravenna to Conway, Pa., near Pittsburgh.

So now we have four police officers standing in a gas station parking lot, looking up at this strange object in the sky. As they watched, the object moved to the northeast. It paused for a moment before moving in a vertical direction at a high rate of speed. It stopped momentarily and then continued moving vertically, eventually out of sight. The Great UFO Chase was over. Looking at his watch, Spaur saw that it was 6:15 a.m., meaning they had been chasing the object for about an hour and fifteen minutes. During that time, he and Neff had traveled roughly eighty-six miles across two states.

The following day, when news of the chase hit the wire, the entire United States quickly became enthralled. How could they not, when multiple police officers claimed to have seen and chased an unknown flying object in the sky? Moreover, after the story broke, more witnesses started coming forward, claiming they had seen the object in the sky. This included Mantua (Ohio) Police Chief Gerald Buchert, who had not only seen the object earlier in the night, before Spaur and Neff did, but was also able to get a picture of it. There are *Men in Black*–type stories about how the moment Buchert went public about having taken a photo of the object, he was contacted by government officials who warned him not to allow the photograph to be published. True or not, Buchert's photo appeared on page 2 of the April 19 edition of the *Akron Beacon Journal*, over the headline "Here's a UFO." It's tough to make out any details in the photo. Suffice it to say that the dark object in the photo appears to have a "half a football" shape, which is what Patrolman Frank Panzanella reported seeing.

Seeking answers about what he and his fellow officers had witnessed, Dale Spaur reached out to Project Blue Book and filed an official report.

POLICE CHIEF SNAPS IT

Ohio Deputies Chase UFO

RAVENNA, O., Apr. 18—(UPI)—"We were close, closer than I ever want to be again," said a deputy sheriff who chased a flying object from Portage county into Pennsylvania.

Hundreds of persons in Ohio and Pennsylvania reported seeing the "brilliant and shiny" object early yesterday morning.

Police Chief Gerald Buchert of Mantua, about eight miles north of Ravenna, said he took a picture of the object from his front yard but the Air Force told him not to release it.

BUCHERT said it looked like "two table saucers put together."

Portage county Deputy Sheriff Dale Spaur said he and his partner, W. L. Neff, "were close" to the object in separate cars and chased it 86 miles for an hour and a half, from near Ravenna to Conway, Pa., near Pittsburgh.

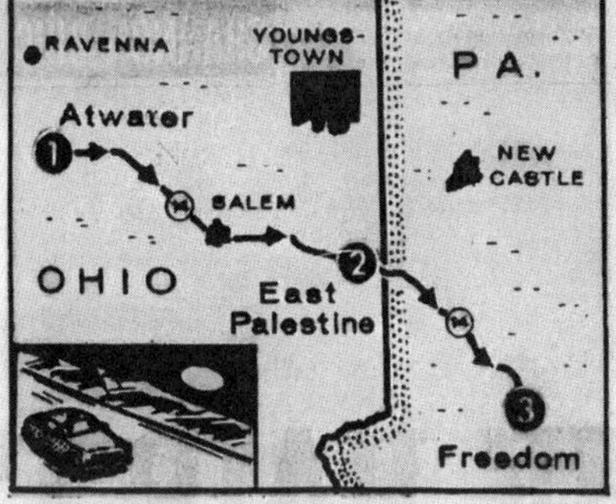

MAP SHOWS PATH OF LATEST OHIO UFO
Deputies Followed Object About 85 Miles—UPI

Spaur said he clocked it at speeds up to 103 miles per hour. From the ground, Spaur said, it looked like the head of a flashlight, about 40 feet wide and 18 feet high.

SPAUR said the lines of the object were very distinct. "Somebody had control over it," he said. "It wasn't just floating around. It can manuever."

The deputy said the chase slowed down near Rochester, Pa., when the cars "got tangled up in a mess of bridges . . . but when I came out from under the bridge it came down and waited for us, just as though it knew these two cars were following it."

"I know nobody's going to believe it, but it's true," he said.

Opposite: Despite being chased for eighty-six miles and across two states, the object has never been identified. *From* The Poughkeepsie Journal Independent, *Monday, April 18, 1966.*

Above: Newspaper article showing just how far the unknown object was followed by law enforcement. *From* The Dayton Daily News, *Monday, April 18, 1966.*

Headquartered at Wright-Patterson Air Force Base, Project Blue Book was designed to investigate reports of unidentified flying objects and determine what people saw and, more importantly, if these objects threatened national security. It officially began in 1952 and had been continually understaffed ever since. By 1966, the unspoken procedure at Project Blue Book was to try to clear as many cases as possible, as quickly as possible. Oftentimes, that meant finding any plausible "natural" explanation, going with that and closing the case. That appears to have been what happened with the Great UFO Chase, as after only a short period, Project Blue Book revealed its findings. Officially, the officers were chasing two objects: a satellite and the planet Venus.

According to Project Blue Book, the object Officers Spaur and Neff first saw and followed was an Echo communications satellite. This was the object they followed into Pennsylvania and what Patrolman Wayne Huston saw when he joined the chase. When the three officers lost sight of the satellite in Pennsylvania, this was because the satellite had moved on. They thought they'd caught back up to it when it reappeared in front of them. But what the officers were really looking at was the planet Venus, which they mistook for the object they were initially following.

Obviously, the officers disagreed with Project Blue Book's findings. If anything, they felt that their collective observational skills were being called into question. There was absolutely no way four trained officers would all misidentify something like that. Satellites don't move like that or get that close to the ground. And planets certainly don't move vertically in the sky, pause and then continue moving vertically until they disappear from view, all in thirty minutes. But that's what they were being asked to believe. So of course, when headlines like "Police Chase Venus Across Two States" started running in national newspapers, people starting poking fun at the officers.

Dale Spaur bore the brunt of the ridicule. The other officers could do a few "no comments" and fade into the background. However, partially because he was the driver of the first chase car, the object became known as Spaur's UFO. This was also partly because Spaur, at least at first, refused to let it go. He just wanted answers, and no one would give them to him. Spaur eventually buckled under all the pressure and ridicule as his health began to suffer. He even felt he needed to leave the police force and Northern Ohio for good. Over the next year, Spaur lost his marriage, his police job and, some would say, his sanity—all because he saw something in the sky that he couldn't explain. Perhaps that's why Spaur told a reporter a mere six months after the Great UFO Chase, "If I could change all that I have done in my life, I would change just one thing. And that would be the night we chased that damn thing. That saucer."

An interesting footnote to this story that speaks to the impact the Great UFO Chase had is that in 1966, Ohio native Steven Spielberg was a student at California State College Long Beach (now known as California State University, Long Beach) studying film. He undoubtedly saw all the newspaper articles about the Great UFO Chase and found it interesting that it occurred in his home state. Perhaps that made him file the incident away, thinking it might make a good movie someday. That day came on November 16, 1977, when Columbia Pictures released his *Close Encounters of the Third Kind*. Early in the film, there's a scene where police officers chase several UFOs across back roads and even over state lines. The scene is clearly an homage to the 1966 UFO chase, even though in *Close Encounters*, the police officers chase UFOs from Indiana into Ohio. In contrast, in 1966, the chase went from Ohio into Pennsylvania. Oh well, that's Hollywood for you!

SELECTED BIBLIOGRAPHY

A-Z Animals. "12 Ohio Cryptids: Appearance, Behavior, and Location." https://a-z-animals.com.

Adkins, Craig. "American Werewolf in Delphos." *Delphos Herald*, October 31, 2006.

Akron Beacon Journal. "Best Bets: Christian Rock Group at Firestone Tonight." June 17, 1978.

———. "Legend of Peninsula Python to Be Celebrated." July 17, 2015.

———. "Python Gets Around, Seen Near Northfield." July 5, 1944.

———. "Where's the Python?" July 12, 1944.

Akron Evening Times. "Ohio's Bloody Bridge." December 10, 1894.

Albert, Barbara A. "Scaring Up Halloween Terror Tales." *News-Messenger*, October 31, 1986.

Albrecht, Brian E. "Baffling History of 2 Indians in Early Cleveland." *Plain Dealer*, June 24, 1990.

Alper, Eric. "History of Barcodes in the Music Industry." That Eric Alper, March 24, 2020. https://www.thatericalper.com

Arnold, Chuck. "Michael Jackson's 'Thriller' at 40: Every Song Ranked from Worst to Best." Billboard, November 30, 2022. https://www.billboard.com.

Bordner, Robert. "The Peninsula Python: An Absolutely True Story." *Atlantic Monthly*, November 1945.

Buchholtz, James. "Let's Talk About Our Town." *Delphos Courant*, August 30, 1961.

Burrough, Bryan. *Public Enemies: America's Greatest Crime Wave and the Birth of the FBI, 1933–34*. Penguin, 2004.

Carey Progressor Times. "Rumors Are False: No Werewolf Here, Police Chief Says." August 9, 1972.

Carpenter, Robert. "Hinkley: Where Buzzards Roost." OhioTraveler.com, https://www.ohiotraveler.com.

Chippewa-Rogues Hollow Historical Society. https://www.chippewarogueshollow.org.

Churm, Steven R., and Carlton, Jim. "Ohio Girl, 13, Found in Southland After 6-Year Search." *Los Angeles Times*, October 23, 1988.

Cincinnati Enquirer. "Map's All He Needs to Start in Digging." July 29, 1951.

———. "Pretty Minnie, the Cook on the Canal Boat." November 25, 1894.

Cincinnati Post. "Dahmer Guilty in Ohio Murder." May 2, 1992.

City of Rittman. "History: Rittman, OH." https://www.rittman.com.

Coleman, Loren. *Curious Encounters: Phantom Trains, Spooky Spots, and Other Mysterious Wonders*. Faber and Faber, 1985.

Cooper, Alecia. "Headless Cyclist Story Gets Better Every Halloween." *News-Herald*, October 31, 1986.

Cummins, Mike. "The Monster Affair." *Crescent-News*, August 9, 1972.

Dahmer, Lionel. *A Father's Story*. Echo Print Books & Media, 2021.

Daily Advocate. "Death Sentence Has Been Decreed for Peninsula Python." June 28, 1944.

D'Annibale, Betsy. *The 1924 Tornado in Lorain & Sandusky: Deadliest in Ohio History*. The History Press, 2014.

Dawidziak, Mark. "Civic's Ghost Vanishes into Thin Air." *Akron Beacon Journal*, October 26, 1997.

Find a Grave. "Find a Grave: Chester Bedell." https://www.findagrave.com.

Findlay Republican Courier. "Defiance Werewolf Sighting Sparks Numerous Reports." August 5, 1972.

———. "Werewolf Reported in Seneca." August 4, 1972.

Fought, Donald. "Librarian's Log: Area haunted by Ghostly Tales." *News-Herald*, October 26, 1978.

Frederick News Post. "Gone but Not Forgotten: Carousel Preservation Groups Hold Conventions." October 9, 1987.

Fuchs, Terry. "Happy Halloween: Ghosts, Goblins and Other Spooky Stuff." *News-Messenger*, October 31, 1981.

Gardner, Erin. "Legend of the Bloody Bridge: Real or Myth?" *Daily Standard*, October 19, 2022. https://dailystandard.com.

Gilbert, Pamela, and Doris Kershner. "Ohio's Castles." *Dayton Daily News*, August 17, 1980.

Gill, Richard. "The Headless Motorcyclist." *Ohio Folklore Society Journal* (December 1972).

Haidet, Ryan. "They're Back! Buzzards Return to Hinkley in Decades-Old Tradition." WKYC, March 15, 2021. https://www.wkyc.com.

Hinckley Township, Ohio. "Township History." https://hinckleytwp.org.

Jackson, James S. "Behind the Front Page." *Akron Beacon Journal*, July 2, 1944.

Justice for Adam Walsh Case Files. "Confession of Jeffrey Dahmer." https://justiceforadam.com/milwaukee.html.

Legg, Jack. *Digging Up Devils: The Search for a Satanic Murder Cult in Rural Ohio*. Pimingee Press, 2023.

Lesie, Michele. "A 'Castle' with an Eerie Past." *Plain Dealer*, October 31, 1989.
MacFarland, Flora. "Look for Your Answer Here: Squire's Castle." *Plain Dealer*, October 9, 1940.
Marion Star. "Buzzards Coming." March 15, 1991.
———. "Suit Over Probe." March 28, 1986.
Masters, Brian. *The Shrine of Jeffrey Dahmer*. Hodder and Stoughton, 1993.
McClelland, Edward. *Folktales and Legends of the Middle West*. Belt Publishing, 2018.
Meatball. "There's a Lost Treasure of Gold in Ohio from the French & Indian War Worth $25,000." WRKR, October 6, 2022. https://wrkr.com.
Miami News-Record. "Unruly Crowd of 20,000 Attends Burial of 'Pretty Boy' Floyd." October 29, 1934.
Miller, Anita. "Elmore Man Plans Special Halloween." *News-Messenger*, October 18, 1979.
Miller, Marilyn. "'Giants of Seville' Get Marker in Village Park. *Akron Beacon Journal*, September 3, 2000.
Mitten, Rayy. "Peeks from Plane Fail to Spot Python's Lair." *Akron Beacon Journal*, July 2, 1944.
———. "Peninsula Python Searchers Find How Sore Unused Muscles Can Get." *Akron Beacon Journal*, June 26, 1944.
Morphy, Rob. "Orange Eyes (Ohio, USA)." Cryptopia, January 14, 2010. https://www.cryptopia.us.
Murphy, James. "Atheist to the End, but Snakes Appeared on Area Man's Grave." *Salem News*, February 27, 1965.
Muskingum Watershed Conservancy District. "Charles Mill Lake Park." https://www.mwcd.org.
News-Herald. "Izzy Sez Do You Remember…" October 2, 1972.
———. "Objects for Collectors." October 11, 1974.
———. "Pair in Search of Spook Light Threatened." June 6, 2006.
News Journal. "Boys Report Seeing Green-Eyed Monster." March 29, 1959.
———. "Ghost Lights in Old Home Mystery to Motor Parties." October 14, 1924.
News-Messenger. "Peninsula Python Changes Locale." July 27, 1944.
———. "Satanic Cult Search Came Up Empty but Left Behind Angry Family, Lawsuit." June 23, 1986.
Norwalk Reflector. "Orange Eyes Mystery Solved." November 19, 1968.
Patton, Virginia. "Tracking the Orange Eyes of Lover's Lane and Other Phenomena." *Norwalk Reflector*, October 30, 1970.
Piqua Daily Call. "Peninsula Python Is Ordered Killed." June 28, 1944.
Plain Dealer. "Obituary: Louisa B. Squire." October 31, 1927.
Richland Source. "What Monster Lurks at Charles Mill Lake?" October 29, 2015.
Richwood Gazette. "Ohio's Bloody Bridge." September 6, 1895.
Sandusky Register. "Carousel Collection Completed by Ziemke." October 5, 1989.
———. "Ohio Bones Were from Dahmer Victim." September 14, 1991.
———. "Spook Light Makes Shift." November 24, 1922.

———. "Well! Well! Here's Ol' Friend 'Spook' Again." September 12, 1922.

Shores & Islands Ohio. "History of Johnson's Island." December 15, 2020. https://www.shoresandislands.com.

Smith, William M. *The Infidel's Grave and Some Strange Incidents About It.* Walfred Publishing, 1956.

Sperber, Ray. "Jottings Off the Cuff: Ann Hayes 'Logical' Choice as Woody's Successor." *News-Herald*, January 5, 1979.

Springfield News-Sun. "New Cleveland Stadium Won't Disrupt Cemetery." October 6, 1991.

Telegraph-Forum. "Again and Again and Again, That Python Shows Up." July 29, 1944.

Uldricks, Rick. "Could Graveyard Across the Street from Progressive Field Play a Role in World Series?" Patch, October 25, 2016. https://patch.com.

UPI. "Eyewitness Tells How 'Pretty Boy' Came to His Death." October 23, 1934. https://www.upi.com.

———. "Grandfather Pleads Guilty in Kidnapping." December 14, 1988. https://www.upi.com.

Wilks, Ed. "No Trace of Monster in Louisiana, Mo. Hunt." *St. Louis Post-Dispatch*, July 19, 1972.

Willis, James A. *The Big Book of Ohio Ghost Stories*. Stackpole Books, 2013.

———. *Southern Ohio Legends & Lore*. The History Press, 2022.

———. *Ohio's Historic Haunts*. Kent State University Press, 2015.

Willis, James A., et al. *Weird Ohio*. Sterling Publications, 2005.

Wolford, Ben. "Seeing a UFO Ruined Dale Spaur's Life." *Portager*, January 9, 2018.

ABOUT THE AUTHOR

James A. Willis has been walking on the weird side of history for over forty years. When not out chasing after all things strange and spooky, Willis has found the time to author over fourteen books, including *Central Ohio Legends & Lore*, *Ohio's Historic Haunts: Investigating the Paranormal in the Buckeye State*, *The Big Book of Ohio Ghost Stories* and *Haunted Indiana*. Willis is also the director of the Ghosts of Ohio, a paranormal research group he founded in 1999.

A sought-after public speaker, Willis has given presentations throughout the United States, where he has educated tens of thousands of people of all ages in crowds ranging from ten to well over six hundred. He has been featured by hundreds of media outlets, including CNN, *USA Today*, *Midwest Living*, *Fox Sports*, the *Canadian Press* and the *Astonishing Legends* podcast.

Willis currently resides in Galena, Ohio, with his wife, daughter and two narcoleptic cats. He can often be found lurking around his virtual abode, strangeandspookyworld.com.